What's Balance Got to Do with it?

Compiled by Heather Andrews

Compiled by Heather Andrews

www.getyouvisible.com

Book cover design by Lorraine Shulba: www.bluebugstudios.com

ISBN: 978-1-989848-11-1

Dedication

To my dear friend Char Loeppky;

Your life was taken too soon. In the short time we knew each other, your impact was felt each day and it affected me deeply. You were my friend and spiritual medium. With your guidance and support I was able to make the change I needed to propel my life forward. The most blessed gift and words of wisdom you shared with me were, "Take care of yourself first always," and, "You have permission to be who you are."

Char, you are missed every day by myself and fellow co-author, Cindy Klamn-Conway.

A quote that reminds me most of you is:

"A friend is someone who gives you total freedom to be yourself." Jim Morrison

You were an incredible gift to me and the world.

Always remembered.

Love, Heather

Gratitude

2020 has been a year of world unification, resiliency, new world balance, and loss during the pandemic.

It is said that, while all of us may have come on different ships to our native land, we are all in the same boat in one world today. Each human has been affected in some capacity by this pandemic.

This book is dedicated to all humans as this left no one untouched.

May you find gratitude for all things once taken for granted.

May you know that we are each responsible for our health and our immunity.

May you be open to new possibilities in wealth and community.

May your faith and spirituality be strong.

May you hold close those you love dearly, and connect from the heart, even if technology is what holds you together.

I am grateful for my co-authors; for their courage to share their stories with the world.

Our hope for you is to read our book with an open heart and use it to guide you on a journey to define balance in your life. May you embrace the peace that can come from knowing it is achievable with ever-flowing ease, and pivot as required to bring balance to your life.

From our hearts with gratitude,

Heather Andrews

Dr. Erin Oksol

Pamela Zimmer

Lily Ahonen

Lisa Berry

Cindy Klamn-Conway

Sarah Konelsky

Monique Feser

Cheryl Hopfner

Allison Tuffs

Susannah Juteau

Table of Contents

Foreword

By Dr. Erin Oksol

I believe success in life is an inside job. I also believe success is individually defined and determined. What works for me may not work for you. So many times, people have come up to me and said, "Wow, Dr. Erin, you must be so busy." I hate the word "busy," and I know hate is a strong word. But busy and I broke up years ago. Who wants to be busy? Have you ever met a young child who says, "I want to grow up and be busy"? I have never met an adult who loves being busy. (Although I have met some who, unfortunately, wear it like a badge of honor.)

When people ask me, "How do you do it all?" I usually answer, "I don't." That gets them curious. When I started my business in 2016, my husband Garth and I sat down and talked about what success looked like to us. It meant giving up the good for the great. It meant we weren't going to buy new furniture but would instead keep the duct tape on the kitchen chairs for a while in order to invest any extra money in the business.

The same was true for our time. We knew I would be investing lots of time into the business, which meant I would have less time for other activities (like cooking and cleaning—ha). I haven't cooked or cleaned my house for over two years. Some would look at my life and say I was failing as a mother or wife. But here's the deal: what works for Garth and me would not work for all couples. My husband and I think we are winning.

Here is what I believe to be true: Balance is not achieved through equal time in all areas but through equal alignment in all areas. The late Maya Angelou said, "Success is liking yourself, liking what you do, and liking how you do it."

I believe true success (and balance) is feeling aligned and fulfilled in all areas of your life. These areas include your family, love, work, relationships, physical health, spirituality, and finances. Instead of seeking equal time in all areas, seek equal levels of fulfillment in all areas. One person's definition of financial success will be different from another person's definition. This is how it is possible, then, for both you and I to report balance in our lives, even when you and I spend different amounts of time in each of the main areas of our lives.

Why is this so important? One of the greatest offenders to your success will be comparing. You comparing yourself to others and others comparing themselves to you. People will question how you spend your time and the price they believe you are paying for your success. If you are unclear about your personal definition of success, you risk missing your own target and hitting someone else's instead.

Pleasing others can easily take over and derail you completely. Your job is to please the people who are important to you, and no one else. You are responsible to establish and maintain your own boundaries. Remember, what other people think of your boundaries is none of your business.

To some, my life would look like a completely imbalanced nightmare. To me, it's my dream life. It works for Garth, our children, and me. What works for you and your inner circle? If you don't define it, someone else will.

This book is written for YOU—to help you discover your own definition of balance. This book will help you design a life that feels truly aligned with your values, mission, and goals. Upon completing this book, I know you will have your own answer to the age-old question, "Is it truly possible to have it all?"

I will leave you with one last thought. What if instead of asking yourself, "Am I doing it right or wrong?" you instead asked, "How's this working for me?"

Go forth and find your own definition of balance. See what works for you. Experiment. Pivot. Extend yourself grace. And enjoy the journey.

Wishing you alignment in all that you do,

Dr. Erin Oksol

https://thepsychologyofmission.com

Introduction

Balance- the true meaning from Webster's dictionary is:

"A state of equilibrium or equipoise; equal distribution of weight, amount etc."

The topic is a huge one, and it's no wonder our overwhelmed society is often at a loss as to whether it's achievable or not.

This book is the third in the series, *What's IT got to do with It?* The first book, *What's Self Love got to do with It?* was published in 2018. As I walked my own journey of feeling worthless after my job restructuring, I discovered that I was not alone. Many women and men struggle with low self-esteem, negative self-worth and don't even realize how harmful it is to their well-being. Having experienced this, observing it on social media and hearing it firsthand in day to day conversations, I decided it was time to bring some stories to the forefront. It is a daily struggle for many.

Quite honestly, it hurts my heart when I think about how we talk to ourselves, and how we put ourselves last in our own lives.

The second book, *What's Money got to do with It?* released in 2019, is about how money mindset can impact our own finances and freedom, and even prevent us from getting out of debt.

The expert authors who contributed to this collaborative book lived the reality of how their own money stories held them back from abundance. They built their businesses from a bare foundation; starting from the bottom and building their expertise in the financial world in order to help others.

When you begin to blend all of the concepts held within these books, the word *balance* really does encompass it all. Balance defines the constant teeter totter effect it takes to keep things in check. In this way, the common thread that runs through all of these book titles is EVERYTHING.

Does the same type of balance work for everyone? No. No person's life is the same as the next, and their balance story is not going to be either.

Balance includes concepts like:

health

wealth

mental well-being

relationships

career

spirituality

self-love

Each co-author has brought to this book a real and raw story to help you understand how unique balance is for each individual. The tools, mindset tips, and lessons learned are shared as a gift to you, our readers.

Each story will focus on one of the above-mentioned concepts. Be prepared to laugh, cry and celebrate how our 11 co-authors pivoted and defined balance in their own lives. Their insights are shared here in hopes that they will help you find your journey to balance, too.

Enjoy!

Heather

Is Balance Possible?
An Expert Opinion

By Pamela Zimmer

It's the age-old question, the big debate, the opinion that divides so many of us good-intentioned, hard-working, purpose-driven human beings. Is balance possible?

To answer this question, we must first understand what it is that we are trying to balance (or not). I'm pretty sure we've all heard about work-life balance, and that, my friends, is exactly the topic of discussion. Whether we work from home, go into a corporate nine-to-five-ish job, or we don't have any kind of formal "work" at all, the work-life balance question is one that constantly haunts us. *Is balance possible?*

I'm just going to jump right in with my expert opinion and tell you *why* I believe what I do. Before I do so, however, I'll briefly let you into my life a little bit so you know who I am and why I'm the one writing this to you. Why does my expert opinion matter so much? Why am I the one with the expert opinion?

As a professional architect of 13 years prior to becoming a stay-at-home mom, I have always been pre-occupied with perfectionism. There was no room for anything less than perfect in my career, and as a new mom it continued to show up. It showed up in trying to be the perfect mom, with the perfect house, hosting the perfect playdate for my kids, having the perfect kids, being the perfect wife, daughter, sister, friend…. you can probably see where that was heading.

The stress of striving for unattainable perfection consumed me. I cared so deeply about what others would think, completely losing myself and any semblance of happiness and peace. Years of putting everyone and everything else ahead of my needs and wants finally caught up to me.

One of the hardest blessings in my life was being diagnosed with severe postpartum depression. It took six years of struggling and fighting through it to learn how necessary it was to stop and take care of myself - to let go of perfectionism, and the need to control it all. These are ongoing lessons, as I continue to practice letting go.

Life wasn't this all-consuming whirlwind powered by my kids at the center of the universe. No, my life was full of different parts and pieces, different people needing and having different places at different times. I was part of that life - my life - and I learned how to weave myself in without dropping all the balls at once.

Oh, trust me, I've dropped plenty of balls in my life so far, and I'm sure there will be more to follow. But now I realize that, like learning to juggle, balance is a practice.

Today, I am a bestselling author of multiple books, an international speaker and your Self-Care Concierge.

Is balance possible? Yes.

There, I said it. You may disagree with me, and you may already be waving your arms in the air yelling at the words on this page, trying to get me to see why I am completely wrong because there is no such thing as balance. Or, you may have just released a big sigh and felt your shoulders drop a few thousand inches from your ears down to a more ergonomically correct location. Either way, it's all good. Either way, please just hear me out.

If we look up the definition of balance, we find this:

verb (used without object), bal·anced, bal·anc·ing.

to have an equality or equivalence in weight, parts, etc.; be in equilibrium

What exactly is supposed to be in equilibrium? Are work and life supposed to be equal? This assumes that there are only ever two "things" to worry about balancing - work and life - and that is perplexing.

Balance is achievable; it's possible. However, balance does not mean equal. Balance is the state of being in equilibrium (according to the definition above), considering there are actually *four* distinct areas to this equation. It's not just work and life - because again, what exactly constitutes "life"?

An article written by Stew Friedman in *Harvard Business Review* states that "The idea that 'work' competes with 'life' ignores that 'life' is actually the intersection and interaction of four major domains: work, home, community, and the private self." I could not have said that better myself, and it one hundred percent supports my theory of four areas of life in which we must experience time in order to find balance.

I identify these four areas as: Home, Work, Social and Self, and together they make up the Permission Pinwheel™. Without going into lengthy explanation, here is a quick breakdown of what each one of those areas consists of:

Home: your family (spouse/partner, kids, etc); your home (where you live/lay your head on your pillow most nights).

Work: your job (whether this is your dream career or three part-time hourly gigs just to make ends meet).

Social: your community (the people you interact with on a regular basis); your inner circle (the people you trust and turn to for advice, support, celebrations and growth).

Self: your person (specifically, your self-care).

Each one of these four areas is important and, together, when we experience time in these areas (not just spend time, but *experience* time - there is a significant difference), this is when we can find balance. When we spend time, we allow it to pass by our conscious awareness without experiencing it. This is like driving to work on autopilot, largely unaware of how we got there. When we *experience* time, we are consciously aware of our surroundings and of our experience as we interact with our environment. This is playing with your children and actually sitting on the floor, creating a Lego masterpiece together.

Earlier, when I stated that "balance does not mean equal, it is the state of being in equilibrium," it is important to clarify that this equilibrium does not come from focusing equal time in each of the four areas. It does not mean six hours each of home, work, social and self. That is unrealistic, and *that* is what I propose by saying balance does not mean equal.

Finding the equilibrium among all four of these areas will sometimes look different year-to-year, month-to-month, day-to-day and even moment to moment. Life is not static, nor are our calendars and obligations.

As a mom of two boys, I know off-the-cuff changes in plans all too well. One kid gets sick or gets a last-minute birthday party invitation. Add to that the planning required for sports practices and games, school performances and recitals, and let's not forget, homework and reading logs. The daily schedule should run like clockwork, right? Wrong!

There isn't a day on earth where the planned schedule runs without a glitch. Do you have kids? Know kids? Been a kid once? Need I say more?

What about those of you without kids? You still have obligations, responsibilities and priorities that I'm pretty certain can, will and do change in the blink of an eye at times.

Perhaps it's that high-paying VIP client who suddenly changes or adds to the scope of work, without changing the deadline. There's a choice you have to make. Without this client your business could fold; they're the bulk of your billing and you believe your financial future depends on their satisfaction and referral. What do you do? Do you sacrifice your mental and emotional health (not to mention potentially damaging your personal relationships) to bend over backward for this client? That doesn't sound like the kind of balance I would recommend to anyone. But hey, that's just me. I've done my time pulling all-nighters and the older I get, the more I realize that unless it's life or death, I'm going to prioritize my sleep!

Could you enroll others to help you (at work and/or at home) so you don't have to shoulder the entire responsibility on your own? Is it a call for all-hands-on-deck? Ultimately, it's your decision. What do you do? Is there a win-win outcome somewhere? What's the cost of your decision? What priorities have to shift?

These are all questions that we have to be willing to answer, whether it's a workplace "emergency" or a true personal life or death family emergency. Something, at some point in our lives, will cause us to re-evaluate our priorities. It might be temporary, or it might be permanent. I guarantee, though, it will shift where you decide to experience your time.

Everything comes down to a choice - your choice. No one else can decide for you what the most important thing is or how to find that equilibrium between Home, Work, Social and Self. Only you can change which area has priority at each given moment.

Here are some other examples of where your priorities might have to shift without prior notice or planning. It's the moments where you have to ask yourself: *what do I do*? You're in the middle of something, adhering to the schedule you set out for yourself, and then life throws you a curveball.

Perhaps it's your best friend who just got diagnosed with breast cancer and she needs you to go with her for her first appointment. You would want her there for you if roles were reversed.

Or perhaps it's your wife calling you from the emergency room because your six-year-old son just fell off the monkey bars at school and broke his arm.

Or perhaps it's something not so personal and completely out of your control, like an accident on the freeway that has you parked in the fast lane longer than you allocated for your drive time.

Or perhaps it's the crazy winter storm that knocked out all the power and you're stuck without wi-fi, unable to upload whatever it is that you desperately need to upload to the cloud.

All of these situations and circumstances force us to evaluate whether we should take time away from one category (one of the four areas) and put time into another category. Do you skip out on your CrossFit class to go with your best friend? Do you let that project sit unfinished on your desk and meet your family at the hospital? Do you turn off the tunes and make sales calls instead while you're stuck on the freeway? Do you renegotiate your timeline and welcome the forced quiet of being off-line?

All of these choices affect our equilibrium and our plan to create and maintain balance. Sometimes this results in just a temporary displacement of time for a few hours, sometimes it's the entire day, sometimes it's longer.

While I understand that there are certain circumstances that are out of our control - like some of the examples mentioned above - how we respond to them are completely within our control. Subsequently, how we adjust and reprioritize are also choices.

Sometimes we can quickly re-adjust and bounce back into our regularly planned schedule. Sometimes we can't. Sometimes, our day becomes the most out-of-whack, unbalanced circus imaginable.

So, what do we do when our best intentions for a balanced day go flying out the window? First thing we do? Breathe. No, seriously, just breathe. Second thing we do? We shift.

Balance is only possible when we know how much weight is in the equation. We all know that a pound of feathers weighs the same as a pound of pennies. But how many feathers would it take to equal the same weight in pennies? It's a give-and-take experiment. Maybe it would take one hundred feathers to equal six pennies. Maybe fifteen feathers would equal two pennies. Until we do the experiment, we won't know. And until we decide how many pennies we are trying to balance with feathers, the equation is impossible to figure out.

Until we know what our priorities are and what the things are that fill us up and bring us joy, the quest for balance is about as pointless as trying to turn the speedometer back by driving in reverse (anyone else thinking of *Ferris Beuller's Day Off*?). We must decide how many pennies are important to us - in other words, we must know what our absolute priorities are.

What do we want? What do *you* want? What are the things that are absolutely non-negotiable? Once we know that (how many pennies), then we can adjust and shift to find the equilibrium (how many feathers).

Everybody is different. There are no two people, families, relationships, work environments or circle of friends that are identical. Not a single one of us will have the same priorities and absolutes as another. That's one of the reasons finding balance is so challenging at times. There's no set formula.

And remember, it's not just having two things to choose between, but four. And it's not simply 6 hours + 6 hours + 6 hours + 6 hours. That is unrealistic.

I wish I could give you the formula. I wish I could tell you how many hours to experience in each one of those four areas. But I can't. And even if I could, each day could be different. Each day is likely to shift to some degree (due to life throwing a curveball, or because your priorities and absolutes and what you want in life has shifted), and that's okay.

I'd like to let you in on a little secret if I may. A secret that, if you follow my advice, will help you find balance. A secret that, no matter who you are, what stage of life you're in, or where you want to go in life, will help you get there. The secret... is to always put yourself first.

Gasp! I know, I heard some of you.

When I say to always put yourself first, I don't ever intend this in a selfish way, but rather in a self-care way. When we take care of ourselves on every level (physical, mental, emotional and spiritual), everything else has a way of working out.

This doesn't mean taking an entire day getting pampered at the spa and expecting that your marriage will miraculously heal itself. This doesn't mean jet-setting off on a six-week vacation and expecting that every project at the office will complete itself on time and under budget. This doesn't mean hiding in a book and expecting your children will cook themselves dinner (well, okay, maybe if dinner is frozen waffles and cereal).

It *does* mean taking regular breaks throughout the day to refuel your body and recharge your mind. It means scheduling in those breaks and holding them sacred. It means waking up in the morning and quietly enjoying your coffee or tea by yourself as you pray or meditate, instead of re-heating it three times because you've served everyone else first and your coffee got cold, once again.

Putting yourself first and practicing self-care is the most important part of this magical un-formula of balance. Why? Because when we are full and happy with joy and love, we are less stressed and more productive, focused and efficient. Practicing self-care gives us the edge on being healthier - physically, mentally and emotionally.

Think about it: if you are happy and healthy the curveballs that life throws at you don't feel so catastrophic. Yes, true, perhaps it is a life or death curveball, but how you respond to it will come from a better starting place. Instead of reacting out of stress, exhaustion, scarcity and fear, you can respond from a place of peace, rest, abundance and love.

Self-care is the permission you give yourself to fill your cup first and pour from the overflow. Self-care is choosing peace, rest, abundance and love over stress, exhaustion, scarcity and fear. Which one sounds better to you?

Making Self (self-care) the priority over the remaining categories (Home, Work, Social) will also give us the clarity we need to have within those remaining categories. When we have more clarity, it's easier to make decisions based on our priorities, and it's easier to know what and how to shift when necessary.

Going back to the question we started with at the beginning - *is balance possible?* - I wonder if you have a stronger or different viewpoint now? My job wasn't to convince you it's possible, although I do hope I've opened your mind to the possibility. My job was to share with you what it takes to achieve balance, understanding that it is a constantly moving target.

Pamela Zimmer

Author, Speaker, Mentor and your "Self-Care Concierge"

Connect with Pamela:
Pamela@PamelaZimmer.com
www.PamelaZimmer.com

Lily Ahonen

Lily Ahonen is a Nurse and caregiver for medically fragile children. She loves to travel and has been to over forty countries. Lily enjoys activities like running with bulls, car racing, rappelling down buildings for charity, and skydiving. She hopes to finish her Private Pilot's License one day. Lily holds the title of Ms. Galaxy Calgary 2020-2021 and was the 2019 National Canadian Ms. Calgary Titleholder. She is an Ambassador for Gems for Gems, assisting survivors of domestic violence, and volunteers with many other local organizations. She is currently working on a Bachelor's degree through Athabasca University and plans to complete a Master's Degree in Equity Studies. She was recently awarded a Makeup Artist Diploma and plans to work in Runway fashion shows internationally.

Connect with Lily:
lilymioc@yahoo.com
https://www.facebook.com/blondvagabond
https://www.instagram.com/ms_galaxy_calgary2020/
https://www.instagram.com/blondvagabond/
Linkedin: Lily Ahonen

Chapter 1:

"No" is a Complete Sentence –
How Building Boundaries Saved my Life
By Lily Ahonen

All too often, we feel the need to change how we live our lives in order to please others and meet society's expectations. We drop our personal needs, goals, and dreams to avoid disapproval. At its worst, the absence of boundaries can lead to toxic relationships with people who are not supportive of our goals and dreams. As women, it can be doubly hard: we struggle to strike a balance between seeing to our own welfare and caring for our children and significant others, meeting the demands of work and our personal commitments, as well as seeing to household tasks. As women, we often feel more obligated to help, be nice, and not say no. This can lead to the neglect of our own needs, the build up of resentment, and, sometimes, a disturbing lack of personal value. This is the story of how I learned the vital importance of boundaries and how it changed my life.

I grew up in a very rough neighborhood; my childhood was filled with struggle and poverty. Twice I was almost kidnapped by strangers. I was always on high alert, like a cornered little mouse on the run from a hungry cat. It was a daily sidewalk occurrence to see men exposing themselves. Walking down the streets, it was common to see people slumped over in alleys, drinking Aqua Velva aftershave or Lysol household cleaner. The streets were littered with dirty mattresses and syringes. Police cars were ever-present, cruising the area. It wasn't unusual to witness S.W.A.T. team members, with their shields and guns drawn, surrounding dilapidated rooming houses and shouting out orders to surrender. I was witness to many fights, shootings, stabbings, and arrests, all before the age of 10.

The first time I considered my own individual needs and set an official boundary for myself, was when I moved out at the age of fifteen. From then on, until I graduated, every day was a juggling act. I had to keep all the balls of attending high school, working, and paying bills in the air. I worked at fast-food restaurants, retail shops, and a car wash. I ended up entering Grade 12 with only twenty-five credits. I needed 100 credits to graduate. I completed seventeen courses during my final year: nine in school and eight by correspondence; the equivalent of two years' worth of classes. I graduated with my class and was very proud of my accomplishment.

I lived downtown and was constantly avoiding predators who were trying to exploit me. I can't even count the number of people who attempted to lure me into a life of drugs, crime, and human trafficking. When I was sixteen, I was hanging out at a nearby café on a Saturday afternoon, drinking coffee on the patio. Two men who were in a biker gang grabbed my arm and tried to forcibly take me with them. I was terrified. The customers at the café intervened to protect me and it turned into a bar brawl type of situation. There was a small pool table in the café and people were fighting with pool cues; pepper spray was deployed. We went to court and the bikers were charged with assault. One of those same men committed murder a few years later.

After high school, I worked two to three jobs for a couple of years before deciding to go to the Southern Alberta Institute of Technology (SAIT) to study Mechanical Engineering Technology. I struggled to finish college. I barely slept, I was working full time hours, and had to leave school twice to help with family commitments. I realize now that I was trying to do too much. I wish I had had the strength to maintain boundaries at that time. I would have graduated on time with much higher grades.

I didn't have many positive role models while growing up; most of the adults I was exposed to suffered from addictions, mental health issues, and lived paycheck to paycheck. I wanted more and was determined to make a better life for myself. The only problem was, I didn't know how. I did not have many examples to follow. I had a very low self-esteem and did not value myself. For most of my life, I had been a caregiver, putting the needs of others ahead of my own. I was incredible in times of crisis: resourceful and creative, always finding a way to save the day and solve any problem that might arise. Despite all of the support I gave others, nobody was there for me in *my* times of crisis. When you are the one that people rely on, the strong one, people don't realize that you also need to be loved and cared for. That you need an ally. On the rare occasions when people did offer to help, I brushed them off saying, "Oh, I'm fine. I'll be ok. I'm used to this." Deep down, I didn't feel that I deserved to receive the same care and support that I gave to others.

I was always very independent; I did my own thing. Yet, I always put others first and reserved only the sparse leftovers for me. I was afraid of disappointing others and my role was so defined that if I didn't put others first, they would guilt trip me and I would feel a deep sense of shame. If I didn't give someone my last dollar to pay their rent, they would be homeless and, yes, it would be my fault. How could I do that to them? Having no answers, I continued to put myself last.

All my life, I had wanted unconditional love and someone who would be my rock. I had wanted to be with someone who wouldn't make me feel like a burden when I wanted my own needs met. I thought I had finally found that when, as a teenager, I became involved in a serious relationship. Here was someone, I believed, who would accept me for who I was, who would support my dreams and goals, someone who would love me. Instead, he became someone who criticized me and made me feel guilty for not being enough. Someone who belittled my dreams and crushed my plans. I wanted him to be what I believed he could be so badly that I kept trying to be better myself. I left him two years later when he hit me. Although I had low self-esteem, physical violence was a deal breaker for me. I knew I deserved better than that.

By the age of twenty-two, I had put myself through college, earning a diploma in Mechanical Engineering Technology. I was proud of my achievement and was looking forward to a career working at field sites. But, the people closest to me did not think that this was a suitable job for a woman, and I found myself going back to school to meet their expectations. After two more years of balancing a full-time school workload and working fifty hours per week, I became a nurse. I gave up my engineering dream to please others; to conform to society's outdated expectations of a woman's place.

Before I got married, I used to travel extensively but I was heavily influenced by people in my life that felt independent travel was no longer suitable for a married woman. I stopped travelling. I wanted to finish the private pilot's license course that I had started as a teenager, but that was too high risk and how could I put myself at risk like that when I was married? I wanted to run with the bulls, go skydiving, and do things that made me feel alive. I dropped all of my boundaries and gave up on all of my dreams to please others.

I truly enjoy being a nurse now, so going back to school to please others was a blessing in disguise. I feel like I have finally found my passion and purpose in life. I work as a nurse for children with complex medical needs. This work is a perfect fit for me because a life of adversity has taught me how to deal with crisis situations, how to keep calm and focused in an environment where the situation is constantly changing. I am taking what I learned from my childhood and using it to help others. I am proud to say that I have found a way to put what some might call "traumatic" experiences to good use.

I changed everything about myself to try to please others so I could finally get the validation I craved and feel worthy. It was never enough. The more I tried, the more demanding the important people in my life became. I had completely lost myself in trying to please others. I neglected myself and felt guilty if I did anything for myself.

The turning point came when I was thirty years old and my daughter was born. That's when I realized the poor example that I was setting for her. It was one thing for people to walk all over me, but there was no way I wanted that for her. I didn't want her to put herself last. I wanted her to always live her life for herself first, to learn how to do what made *her* happy and not just live off the leftover scraps as I had done. I knew that I had to change my relationship with boundaries if I was going to be the good role model I wanted to be. I had to be strong for her, so she would grow up to be confident.

It was during that first year of motherhood that I began to set boundaries. I now had a family and a child that I needed to put first. I started to say no to external demands on my time and money. I stopped taking on the role of fixer for other people's problems. I was simply floored by all of the negative responses I got for setting what I thought were reasonable boundaries. One person stopped talking to me for two years and blamed me for all of the troubles in their life, all because I was unwilling to cover their bills as a result of some bad choices they had made. I started to learn that I was not responsible for the choices that other people made, I was only responsible for myself. I was also not responsible for their anger towards me; I had done nothing wrong and I was not the cause of their misfortune. A big part of maintaining my boundaries was learning to separate what actions and reactions belonged to me, and what belonged to others.

Even though my boundaries with the outside world were strengthening, my sense of self was still being trampled on at home. Three years after my daughter was born, I realized I was an empty shell. Before I got married, I had been full of hope and excitement. I approached life with a sense of adventure and wonder. But afterward, I just got used to pretending to be someone else in order to make my marriage work. Some friends noticed and were horrified. I was so beaten down that I was just existing, not living. Once again, my daughter was my catalyst for courageous change. I could not bear for her to grow up with a mother who was weak and not living her authentic life.

After two years of counselling and countless attempts to salvage my marriage, I made the decision to leave. I was scared. I had zero confidence in myself and didn't believe I could make it on my own. This from someone who had lived alone since she was fifteen, put herself through high school and college, travelled to over forty countries, and lived abroad in four of them.

I realized that nothing could be worse than the hell I was living in at the time: not able to be myself, feeling trapped and alone. I decided to leave and, instantly, I felt at peace. The first year was extremely difficult; I had left with only one hundred dollars in my pocket and no couch. I worked very hard over the next two years and I managed to buy two properties by myself. I was never more thankful for my education, which allowed me to have a well-paying job that I love.

I still struggled with low self-esteem and was still a people pleaser. I slowly began to do things for myself but still felt guilty about doing so. Over the next couple of years, I learned that I needed to put myself first in order to give to others without burning out. I learned that it was okay to have my own needs met. I began to travel again and to buy new clothes. I had always wanted braces to fix my teeth and to go to the gym but had been told that I was vain for wanting those things. I felt guilty for trying to improve myself and I didn't feel like I deserved it. I did end up getting braces and I also completed a fitness program that helped me lose weight and become stronger.

Life was going really well, I felt at peace and was very happy. Then, in 2015, the bottom suddenly fell out. I suffered a horrible back injury. I lost my job and had to leave my home, rent out my house, and move to a cheaper apartment. My back injury became worse and I ended up with paralysis in my leg. I was hospitalized for close to a month. I had back surgery a few months later and recovered fully, but, a few weeks after my surgery, one of my houses flooded and I felt that I might have reached my breaking point. Nevertheless, I gathered up my strength and, with help of friends, I made it through the renovations. I was able to rent the house to new tenants a month later. All of these struggles made me stronger and helped me to realize that I was capable. I looked back on everything I had been through and what I had accomplished, and I knew that I could make whatever kind of life I wanted for myself. I realized that my life was mine, that I could live for *me*, and that I didn't need to care about what other people thought. I lost many friends during that time as I had changed from a "Yes Woman" into someone with boundaries.

I had wanted my daughter to have a strong role model, someone who could take on challenges and overcome them. Someone who could live a fearless life and take risks. I had succeeded. Seeing all of the obstacles I had overcome, made me realize that I was capable of really anything. I now had indisputable proof.

I began to associate with a new group of people who were positive, accountable, and lived their lives to the fullest. I was no longer being drained by negative people who blamed others for their misfortunes. Through listening to inspirational speakers, I began to understand that it was possible to change my story and that my past did not define me. I became my own hero, changing my own life through healthy boundaries. Every single day was a chance at a new start. When I committed fully to what was important for me and my family, I discovered that there was no limit to what I could achieve. I will always live my life in service to others, but now I know to put myself first. Boundaries and balance allow me to give freely without incurring any detrimental effects.

I am sharing my story so others can know it's never too late to rewrite your future. Every single day is the chance for a fresh start. I feel like I've woken from the dead; like I'm alive again.

Since my divorce, I've started to travel again. I've run with the bulls at the Strathmore Stampede, not once, but twice. I almost got a horn in the butt the last time, but I came out in one piece. I've gone skydiving again. I've rappelled down a 30-story building for charity three times, raising a total of $4500 for Easter Seals. I own two properties. I also have the career of my dreams: I am still working as a nurse and have found that it is my true passion.

My main focus right now, is to be the best mother I can be to my children. I want them to see someone who sets goals and then takes action to make them happen. I make sure that I have my own life as well. Being fulfilled helps me to be a better mother and have more to give of myself to my children. It is easy to burn out when you constantly put others ahead of yourself. Balance is important. My life is full with work, volunteering, and fun experiences. Some people keep busy to avoid dealing with difficult feelings and life's challenges, but I am not hiding, I am making up for lost time. I don't want to miss anything anymore. At one time, all of my dreams were squashed and now is my time to go after them.

Living your authentic life is not just a "might do," it's a *must do*. It's *your* life. People will judge you no matter what you do, so you might as well do what you are called to. The most freeing thing is to live your life without caring about what others think; it is like being let out of a life-sentence in the tiniest prison in the world. Like me, many people live their lives trying to conform to a standard they think they *should* live by, trying to live up to the expectations of their friends, family, and society. I've learned to say no. I don't take on what I am not responsible for and would impact my life negatively. I work hard and sacrifice for what's important to me, without guilt.

I want people to know that even coming from a background of poverty and abuse, you have the power to change your story. You can set boundaries for what you accept, knowing that you don't have to live with abuse.

It is important to find a good support system and have a sense of community in order to build and maintain your boundaries and reach your goals. Balance means having healthy relationships and supports. They form the foundation needed to give you the confidence to live a life with healthy boundaries and to feel secure to live your most authentic life.

Don't be afraid to make changes at any time in your life; life is not a rock, it's a river. It is essential to say no to things that will overwhelm you and that don't add value to your life. You must stop living your life for other people; your best life can't start until you do. Be yourself. Live for yourself. Be YOU.

Lessons Learned:

1. When making decisions, if it doesn't align with your beliefs and values, has the potential to cause harm to you or others, or is illegal - 'No' is a complete sentence. You don't need to justify your decisions to anyone.
2. Find a support system of people who are positive and encouraging, healthy role models to guide and advise you and help you find your path: people who can offer a reciprocal relationship and unconditional emotional support.
3. Let go of wanting people to like you and approve of you. Your job is not to please others, your job is to please yourself.
4. Other people's actions and reactions are not your responsibility. The only things you should care about are the ones you have control over – your own thoughts, actions and reactions. Put your focus there and let the rest go.
5. Make sure you have time for yourself. Help others when and where you can, but not at the expense of your own wellbeing. Make sure you and your family have enough time, money and support first, then give any extra to those you want to help. (see #1 for decision making)
6. Find out what is most important to you and your family and put your energy there first.

A-ha Moments and Self-Reflections

Note your Thoughts

_____

_____

_____

_____

_____

_____

_____

_____

_____

_____

_____

_____

_____

_____

_____

_____

_____

_____

_____

_____

Lisa Berry

Lisa Berry is an expert in breathing life into the dreams of authors who want to express their stories and messages vibrantly and energetically through being interviewed and interviewing. A #1 best-selling author, she is also a successful international radio show host and podcaster.

As a writer, Lisa draws on her own experience to create short stories that she offers up to her readers as "coachable moments" in the hopes of making an uplifting and life-affirming connection with them, whatever their circumstances.

As a host, she creates space for conscious conversations that are broadcasted globally, which promotes worldwide holistic happiness and connection. She also coaches other show hosts on how to deliver exceptional experiences to their audiences by helping them to produce individual podcast episodes as well as entire series.

Using wellness for all as her guiding star, Lisa's life passion is to find, help, and connect with those who need and want to shine.

Connect with Lisa:
www.lightonliving.com

http://omtimes.com/iom/shows/light-on-living/
https://www.facebook.com/lisa.berry.LOL
https://www.linkedin.com/in/lisaberry1/

Chapter 2:

Barefoot Balance:

Getting a Grip on What Serves You

By Lisa Berry

An hour-long drive in Toronto traffic, very tricky parking, and all the anticipation of taking the first step toward transforming my entire life in this very session, and my first lesson was on standing?

This could not be right; I knew how to stand, or did I?

I won't keep you in suspense: I did *not* know how to stand; at least not in a way that gave me power, that felt effortless, that actually brought me comfort and ease.

Remember when you were a little kid and you had to be somewhere with your parents, or do something at school, and you had to stand for way longer than you wanted? And your body just started to fail you? You'd start crumpling up and get cranky and ornery and tired?

Well, when I learned how to stand in this magical way, I discovered that now I had the power to make all of those uncomfortable physical and emotional feelings disappear! From that day forward, I knew how to generate stability, steadiness, and balance in all areas of my life. I compensated and adjusted when external factors threw me off all from re-learning how to stand.

Posture as a Window into the Self

Posture was something my mom was always on us girls for. I thank her now for all, and I do mean *all,* those times she poked us or sharply said, "sit up"; but, boy oh boy, it was hard work. Perfect posture gives you a better appearance, is better for your physical health, and improves your breathing; but, to achieve and hold that noble stance, there are muscles that need to be strengthened, poor habits that need to be dropped, and an alignment that needs to happen.

I'm always amazed by the power of "standing tall," the strength that comes from being in a beautiful upright position. I'm also acutely aware of the loss of power, the decreased energy, and the negative shift in my own emotional balance when I slouch.

Slouching is a side effect, a symptom, a tell-tale sign of your wellbeing and vibration. Think about a time when you were excited, you heard happy news, or you were on your way to a highly anticipated destination. Can you remember how tall and strong you were standing? Or even sitting? You felt so tall that you could just reach up and touch the stars, and your body would show it. Now imagine, aargh, receiving bad news: a radio announcement of unexpected heavy traffic on your way home, the cancelation of an event, a lottery ticket you thought was a winner but isn't. What is it that immediately happens? You drop, you slouch, you lose the energy to hold yourself up.

Let's go even deeper with that idea: Imagine that you're living a life filled with disappointment, sadness, unfulfilled dreams, physical tiredness or pain, discontent with your career or the social circle you've chosen. Those feelings can hold you in a crumpled, low, and disempowered posture.

The great news is that, while feelings can affect your posture, your posture can also affect your feelings. You really can shift into a confident, energized, and happier state of mind by simply adjusting your posture. If you allow your breath to flow through you and calm your nervous system, if you allow the balance of your physical self to float and expand, you can use your body to help stabilize and balance out your emotional state. With regular practice, Barefoot Balance can actually re-establish your wellbeing.

Now, surely, I had *walking* down pat, right? I not only had decades of good old-fashioned walking experience, I even thought I might have an edge seeing as I had taken modelling lessons, been up on the runway a few times, and repeatedly practiced both high-heeled and fashion footwear struts. Again, no suspense here, I did *not* know how to walk, at least not in a way that generated and circulated a life force through me with every step. In a way that positioned my heart to beam out love and prepare me to be in a state ready for receiving. A way to walk that positioned my eyes so I would see the world's beauty as I made a connection with mother nature and other beautiful creatures.

Re-pouring My Foundation

In order to regain my balance on an energetic level, I needed to get a grip on how I was living my everyday life, right down to my very structural positions.

My daily life was filling up with *so* many little things that upset me or made me unhappy that they were beginning to have a negative impact on me. A pimple one day, my car not starting the next, a client not showing up for a session, the internet connection going down, bills coming in left, right and centre, a fight with my boyfriend. These are "normal," everyday occurrences, but I was dealing with them negatively. I wasn't coming from a place of self-love, in fact I was being really hard on myself; even kind of mean. I called myself "ugly" when I saw the pimple, I felt "poor" because I had an older car, I felt "disrespected" when a client missed a session, I got angry and started ridiculous explanations for my internet problems, and I didn't feel worthy of love when I had a fight with my guy.

But it wasn't just the little things that were adding up. You see, back in 2009, I was on my fifteenth attempt at making a home in less than ten years. Stability seemed impossible for me.

My life had become positively anorexic, as the bags I lugged around with me got lighter with every move. I figured that the less stuff I had, the more I could control it, the less I would have to lose and, by extension, the less I would be hurt. But, that kind of weightlessness isn't grounded and doesn't really feel safe.

Here I was, a published writer, a regular television guest and contributor, as well as an established holistic nutritionist and life coach; but I was lonely, hopeless, and depressed. There was no *Om* in my life, I had pinched myself off and was so far out of balance that stability, connection, and happiness were light years away, if not totally out of reach. I had been hiding, shrinking away, hunching my shoulders to protect my heart; bowing my head down from the feeling of brokenness, helplessness, and depression. My disconnection showed in my posture.

Slowly, I began to identify with the idea of "having nothing but myself" but along with it came the dichotomy of enjoying the freedom while suffering and mourning each move like a death and failure. Selfish, withdrawn, and scared, I pulled away from everything. Simultaneously, I desperately and fruitlessly tried to grasp for anything that might offer a sense of control. It became clear that I would have to gain true control over my life to serve my highest self, which I could sense was still in me somewhere. During that dark period, I'm not sure I believed that I'd ever see the light. When I say "see the light" I am referring to my own light. I was so dim, so sad. There was no joy, no ray of light or life beaming from me.

What I soon learned, is that it wasn't a vicious circle that I was stuck in, it was in fact a long ugly chain of negative emotions all linked together in a straight line. I needed to start re-forging it into a beautiful loving chain, one link at a time.

A belief is a thought that we've repeated so many times in our minds that we've come to accept it as truth. We now operate or act from that belief (thought). I went back to basics and realized that by starting my day off in a slouch, a defeated stance, an uninspired, reclusive posture, I was more likely to respond to everything in my life with the corresponding attitude. So, I went for it! I put into practice the daily habit of Barefoot Balance. Everyday, I started out standing tall, feeling firm and confident, allowing the effortless flow of breath to come and go so I could give and receive. I wish I had learned this practice so much earlier in my life.

From Dim to Shiny

What helped me to harness that very sense of believing I could indeed step into my highest power, was the inspiration I received from the up-lifters, teachers, and role models I found on the Internet *and* that 90-minute yoga session where I learned how to stand on my own two feet, with my entire body and soul.

My focal point, my goal, was no longer to find the right home or the right relationship, it was to nurture, grow, and experience life in the now. Piercing through my darkness and shining light on what would become my stable and trusted path, was my connection to my *Om*. My sacred *Om* where all things I manifested began in vibrational form (*Om* is the most elemental vibration and has one origin of being a seed sound, where all things manifested began in vibrational form and continue to contain that frequency).

I could never have seen it coming. In a single moment, with one breakthrough, my life changed in a big positive way for the second time. I learned how to stand. I learned how to *be.* I learned how to allow life-force to flow through me and to feel energized at the same time! The breakthrough I experienced was a realization that what I needed was "choice and responsibility for my highest self" and that that started with how I stood physically, what I stood for personally, and how easily I could do both when I was aligned with my inner self. This connection between our physical bodies and our emotional states, when balanced, is truly effortless. It's weightless and pleasurable.

Stacking Stance

I'd love for you to experience it, and here's an easy exercise you can try. I call this the 'Stacking Stance'. Did you ever play with blocks? Stacking one block on top of another to build the highest tower that you could? Not all of the pieces were the same size but you found that you could lean one block a little this way and shift another block a little that way. Do you remember that your first, grounding, foundational block was *always* centered? What about the monkey chain game? Well that first monkey always had to be secure as he swung about. Finding the centre in your own physical balance can also help you to experience effortless, powerful, and trustworthy balance in your mental and emotional areas of life.

To do the Stacking Stance follow these steps:

A. Get barefoot.
B. Comfortably plant your feet on the ground, about hip width apart and balanced with a little more weight in the heels than the toes.
C. Tilt your pelvis slightly by tucking in your tush; you'll feel relief on your lower back.
D. Pull back your shoulders to open up the chest and heart area, and stand nice and tall, not bending forward or backward.
E. Pull down your shoulder blades and drop your shoulders away from your ears.
F. Tighten your quadriceps, your thigh muscles, as if you're pulling them off of your kneecaps.
G. Soften your face muscles, forehead, jaw. Relax your eyes and eyelids to a low gaze but leave them open slightly.
H. Find the balancing point of your head on your neck. Let it wobble around til it feels like it's floating.
I. Exhale, then slowly breathe in your nose and out through your mouth as if you were blowing through a straw.
J. Expel all your air until you feel your abdominal (tummy) muscles engage then hold the contracted position until you breathe in your next breath comfortably.
K. Notice the blood drain from your arms to fill your fingertips that have most likely been elevated all day while working.
L. As you find yourself stacked beautifully, you'll simply be in pure balanced form, effortlessly erect, and exerting minimal energy.
M. Enjoy this peaceful posture for a few moments and as often as you can.

Coming Back to Life

Learning to stand barefoot was absolutely the perfect place for me to start harnessing my feelings of "groundedness," connection, and, more importantly, safety! It gave me back my *balance*; allowed me to feel the gifts locked inside me. My Barefoot Balance brought me back to life.

The way that balance has impacted my life so far, is that it has secured and steadied me for almost ten years, now, in the same "home": my sacred *Om*, which is always with me and always welcomes company. Barefoot Balance has supported my heart's balance.

What I learned in that first yoga lesson, was that balance is a person's perfect state of being; one that is effortless and allows flow. One that feels good, even pleasurable.

Allow your authentic state of being to shine through, explore which core values and beliefs might be in conflict with each other, and which ones are serving you, so you can live your life as your highest, best self. Use the Stacking Stance to experience your Barefoot Balance and feel the ease with which opportunities arise for you to create a rejuvenated and balanced life.

Lessons Learned:

1. How we stand reflects how we are feeling in the moment. Our posture tells a story, a tale of attitude, beliefs, daily practices, and connections.
2. We can use our awareness of our physical presentation and use its power to remain in balance.
3. As we become clearer on what serves us, on what feels good and is effortless for our bodies, our goals become much easier to define as well as achieve.
4. To be out*standing* we need to stand out by living with passion. Standing in a balanced and grounded manner supports our heart and promotes our breathing. It also keeps us stable and unshakable.

Mindset Tips:

1. Posture affects mindset and state. The world throws stuff at us all day long and self- correction is us choosing a better way.
2. Do regular posture checks, to empower, love, nurture, and motivate yourself.
3. Get back on track with your goals and/or get back into alignment with your beliefs, by adjusting your posture.
4. To restore energy and lift spirits: lift your head, so your chin is parallel to the ground, and look up.
5. To lessen stress and anxiety: drop your shoulders, breathe deeply and slowly.
6. To relieve overwhelm: tuck in your tush and tighten your abdominals to relieve low back pressure.

A-ha Moments and Self-Reflections

Note your Thoughts

_____

_____

_____

_____

_____

_____

_____

_____

_____

_____

_____

_____

_____

_____

_____

_____

_____

_____

_____

_____

_____

Monique Feser

Monique Feser is an Optimization Health and Life Coach. Her passion is helping people optimize every aspect of their lives to achieve meaningful change for the better.

She believes that positive change comes from finding balance in three key areas: the body, the mind, and money matters. Starting with the four foundational pillars of happy, healthy, sexy, and wealthy, she encourages clients start by focusing on internal transformation in order to obtain the changes they seek in the outside world.

To fulfill her dream of being a catalyst for transformational change, she founded Happy Healthy Sexy Wealthy Inc., a company that embodies her philosophy of change and offers all of the tools necessary for her clients to achieve the results that they seek.

Monique starts by asking, "What would your happy, healthy, sexy, wealthy life look like?" and then works together with her clients to help them create the life they desire.

Connect with Monique:
www.moniquefeser.com
https://www.facebook.com/monique.feser
https://www.instagram.com/monique.feser/

Chapter 3:

Balance Schmalance!

By Monique Feser

It's a chilly winter day in November and I've just sat down after working all day on my business. Building my Happy, Healthy, Sexy, Wealthy Inc. brand is no small task, there are a lot of moving parts. I not only engage in life and health coaching *per se*, I also spend time promoting the nutritional program of a separate global company, take part in speaking engagements, and mentor others. My passion to help people live a full, balanced, and healthy life is time consuming and requires me to be constantly connecting with new people, many messages, emails, and managing my social media. Thankfully, unlike many people, I absolutely love social media, it gives me the opportunity to use my creative mind. Some of my favourite business activities include helping driven, inspired team members to grow their own businesses, and assisting one-on-one coaching clients to achieve clarity and alignment with their health and wellness needs. When someone says, "You are in an inspiration" or, "You make me want to keep going," it fills my heart.

At the end of a day like today, I am tired but content. I arrive home and feel such a sense of accomplishment and pride. Sitting on the couch, working on my laptop in front of the fireplace in my new home designed and decorated by *moi,* the house feels so completely like my own, you know what I mean? It gives me a feeling of freedom because everything is exactly how I want it. It just feels like me. The man of the house, my husband and partner, Rob, is cooking dinner (chicken stir fry with peas and mushrooms, it smells delicious.) We do our very best to eat a healthy, well-balanced diet so we can have many years together.

Years ago, I could never have imagined that this would be my life. There was a time when I could barely pay the rent; now, I own three houses. I always pictured a life where I was financially secure, successful, independent, at peace with myself, and happy, but I had no idea how to get here. Where is here? Today I am a Certified Health and Life Coach, and I have built a marketing team of close to 300 people and growing. My passion is helping others create the life that they have always imagined. Some need help getting their health back on track; for others it's their finances. As my mentor says, "we build bodies and bank accounts." It is a joy to help and inspire others to grow from where they are to where they want to be. Just like I did.

The most important transformation I have experienced in the past fifteen years, however, isn't in my career. The biggest change happened in my mind. I could never have created the life I have now if I hadn't changed my self-defeating mindset and freed myself from caring too much about what other people thought. There can be no life balance if expectation and judgement run your mind. And run my mind they did, limiting my joy and poisoning my relationships. Until, that is, I put on my big girl boots and kicked my expectations to the curb. In this chapter, I'm going to share where, why, and how I created the life of my dreams.

Back when my current life was an unimagined dream, I was a hardworking young woman in my twenties. I had zero balance. Pedal to the metal *all* the time. That meant going to college, working at least one job, if not two or three, and partying as much as I could afford. At that time, what drove me was need. I needed money to live. My family is large and wonderful. I would occasionally receive a generous gift from my parents, but for the most part I needed to fend for myself. I was a completely free spirit; I did what I wanted when I wanted. Like a fairly typical twenty-something, I never wanted to say no to my desires. I wanted to travel, whoop it up, have nice things, and so on. But the necessities of life usually got in the way. Going to college and holding down several jobs meant that I was busy most of the time. I dated and spent time with friends as much as I could. I smoked, although I was never really good at it, and often drank too much. I was taking my health and my body completely for granted.

By my late twenties, I started to feel the effects of my lifestyle and decided that it was time to find more balance, which at the time I equated with a "traditional" life. So, I found a husband, gave birth to two great kids, bought a house, and worked at a 9-to-5 job. However, having achieved the traditional life I thought I wanted, I still felt unfulfilled. I didn't have a clear vision of what it was, but I always knew there was something wonderful just waiting for me to discover. Eventually, I put myself out there in the corporate world and was rewarded with a "reputable" job. It took someone who knew nothing of my past to see me as a capable and talented woman. I remember that, initially, when I was applying to be a legal assistant, I was constantly turned down because of my lack of experience. Well, you can't get experience if no one will hire you! Finally, I offered to work for free at one small firm, even though I really couldn't afford it. I guess they thought I was showing initiative, so they hired me and paid me too. Once I had my foot in the door and felt respected by my co-workers and the lawyers I worked for, there was no stopping me. After that, I just kept advancing. I was so proud of myself. No more cowboy boots, shorts, t-shirts, and slinging beer for me. It was a new life of pumps, skirts and generally looking and feeling professional.

In my late thirties I suddenly found myself facing a Mount Everest-sized challenge. You see, even though I was married with two children, I was doing everything alone. I was lonely and single parenting within my marriage. When I fully realized what my situation was, I thought, *then why not be alone?* At thirty-six, I struck out on my own and embarked on what would be my existence for the next ten plus years. When I got divorced, that's when shame started running things. I didn't know it at the time. It crept into my world slowly and I was too busy to notice the deep impact it would have on my life and how it would affect my inner wellbeing.

Life as a divorcee and single parent turned into a massive lesson in letting go and finding *my* balance. Not what friends and family thought balance should look or feel like, but what balance meant to me and my kids. Six months into the divorce and my single parenting adventure, my ex-husband moved to another province over eight hours away. From then on, I really was on my own. With very little financial support at first, and living in a rented townhouse, I was up every morning with my three-year-old boy, who didn't like to sleep through the night, and my little four-year-old girl with a speech delay. Every weekday morning, I was the one who got them up, fed them breakfast, and took them to daycare and/or playschool. I then went to my very demanding full-time job as a real estate paralegal. Except for every couple of months, when their dad would visit, I was the only point of contact for my kids, twenty-four hours a day, seven days a week. I remember once saying to the kids, "only seventy-nine more sleeps till you see Daddy." It broke my heart. Broke my back too. So much responsibility on my own: no family nearby and no friends because we had only been in the city for a year. Finally, I reached out and found a supportive group of other single parents to plan activities and eventually trade babysitting with.

For the next ten years, my life was completely consumed with being a mom while trying to be a powerhouse of a woman too. All parent-related activities fell on my shoulders: dentist, doctors, volunteering at the school, snack days, activity and craft organizing, soccer, cubs, Guides, basketball, among other things. Add to that, staying fit, keeping the kids engaged in school, and taking them to the library, or sometimes to Chapters, to read the books for free so I could spoil them with an apple juice and get myself a latte. In those ten years we learned to love our trips to the thrift store, mostly Value Village which was pronounced "Valoo Valage" to make it sound fancy. It was fabulous fun. Everyone got an outfit and a toy for under $50 total. We enjoyed any free or low-cost activities we could find, like walks in Fish Creek Park or going to the cheap-seats movie theatre with $2.00 matinees. Garage sales were also a favorite.

My life was consumed by the pre-Facebook equivalent of "shaming". Rightly or wrongly, I felt judged everywhere I went. Trying to live up to so many expectations, only created greater chaos in my life. I needed to get off the merry-go-round. If I didn't let this shit go and start living my life without worrying about what other people thought, I would slowly go crazy. Sometimes it felt like I was already halfway there. I had to learn to trust my own judgement instead of allowing myself to be consumed by everyone else's opinion. It made me feel sick to my stomach to think that I couldn't make anyone happy, so why do it? Why not just worry about me and my own instead?

Whether it was the result of external pressure, or was internally generated, expectation had a terrible hold on me. A memorable example self-generated expectation was *George's* mom. On every special occasion, every holiday, my son would come home from school with the most perfect little snack or gift from *George's* mom. Oh, how I despised that woman despite never having met her. I imagined her in a cute little cardigan, hair in a fashionable messy bun, perfect skin, and super fit because she had all the time in the world to work out. Basically, in my mind, she was everything I thought I should be as a mom and a wife; but my reality was nothing like hers. I didn't have the time to be the perfect mom. I was the mom who needed to drop my kids off at daycare for someone else to take them to school because I didn't have time to do it myself. I was the mom who only showed her face at school when one of the kids vomited or worse. I didn't bake. I picked up store bought cupcakes and put eyeballs on top for Halloween or hot lips for Valentine's day. On Valentine's Day, *George's* mom created perfect little bags with a heart on each and a sprinkle or glitter covered homemade cookie inside. You get the picture. I was *not* George's mom.

The feeling of not being "enough" and of being constantly judged carried over into every area of my life. I had assumed that living in a large city would give me anonymity, that no one would care about what I said or did. Amazingly, I could still feel the pressure. I could feel it because it wasn't coming from outside, it was coming from inside me. I was totally committed to my children but, as a single parent, I had to handle that two-person job on my own and I had high expectations of myself in that regard. I have always taken a ton of pride in providing my children with everything they need, but, at the beginning, I struggled a lot. I was on my own with two little kids under five years old. How could I meet the expectations I had set for myself, much less contend with the judgement of others? Nevertheless, I was also constantly being measured against the opinions of those close to me. Friends and family can be among the harshest of critics and I had a hard time standing up to them; I still do at times. It was tough dealing with the people who couldn't help but cast their Judgey McJudgerton opinions my way.

Some of the most painful judgements, the ones that pierced me like daggers, were the ones that echoed my own fears. Imagine receiving an email from a loved one and being told that you couldn't possibly survive alone as a divorcee, that you must have a man involved to succeed, that you were being unbelievably selfish, and that you simply weren't strong enough to make it on your own. This broke me. I read it and wept. I took a few deep breaths, read it again and then deleted it for good. I could not endure reading that meanness and negativity again. Part of me believed it and part of me wanted to tell the author to go to hell. Neither was right. At that moment I told myself that I would prove myself to everyone, that I would and could do this on my own with *no* help from a man. I failed to consider how difficult it would be.

Fast forward several years later, only to hear that same person tell me that "oh, look, you buy designer clothes, but your children go without." That one cut deep too. I was still being judged by what was on the outside. Where I used to be judged for being a young blonde with a good body and fair-sized bust, now I was being judged for what I wore. I just couldn't win! I had to remind myself not to feel guilty for the nice things we had. No one knew how many trips we had taken to Valoo Valage in previous years, so they couldn't appreciate the hard work that went into now being able to afford a few treats.

Even though I was proud that I was excelling in my career while single parenting, I still had to contend with what seemed to be an endless stream of guilt. Imagine my employer telling me that I was "a pathetic single mother" after I had been with him for six years. I often had to bring my kids to work and get them to rest on the dirty office floor while I worked late, or had to drag them to the office with me when they were sick, so I could pick up files to work on at home. I took such pride in my job and in taking good care of my children, so to be told by my boss that I was "pathetic" and that he "felt sorry for my kids" just broke my heart. It made me feel like a complete loser. When he said these cruel things, I broke down and cried right there. I tried to answer, to fight back, but I couldn't. All I could do was cry and I hated myself for it. It made me feel weak. It made me look even weaker in the eyes of someone who already thought I was. There were many more instances of hurtful words. Despite all of the trials and tears, I knew in my heart of hearts that I would rise up and be a strong woman, but first I had to cry a bit.

A huge reason that expectation had such a strong hold on me was guilt. I guess I would say that the guilt of leaving the kids' father is what drove me to try so hard to give them everything a two-parent family had: a house, any and all activities that they wanted, vacations, and a "dad" or father figure (this proved to be quite a difficult task). Another reason was that getting a divorce meant that I had to give up my old life. Why would that be so hard, if I am the one who chose to divorce? Well, I had to give up the life I had planned for, the one I expected. When I was younger, I had planned to have children, to be a wife and a mother. With the divorce, my situation changed; I was always going to be a mom, but I was no longer anyone's wife. In giving up married life, I was letting go of what I, up to that point, I had believed I needed: security. I was letting go of the persona that I had created for myself in my mind, and what I had always imagined would be the perfect life. On some level, I was punishing myself for not living up to those old expectations. I see now that I doubled down on pushing myself to be the perfect mother I thought I should be to make up for all the guilt and insecurity I was feeling.

As a result of feeling all of this pressure, judgement, and expectation, I was always searching for approval from someone. Anyone. I was a good mom, but I don't think I was always present for my kids when I needed to be. I had so much to do and so many appearances to keep up, that I missed out on the joys of life more often than I should have. I wanted to "have it all," so I worked hard and kept climbing the ranks to a better job, better pay, better hours, better benefits, but my health suffered. When I was thirty-five, I threw my back out while kneeling to pick up one of the kids; I was also skinnier than I'd ever been because I didn't eat. I just didn't take care of myself properly. I was running around from morning to night with the kids, my job, and dating (sometimes more than I should have). I wasn't taking the time to engage in self-care. Was I happy? At times, but it was more about situational happiness than over all contentment.

I had to let go of expectation if I was ever going to be happy, fulfilled, and truly joyful. I could feel myself growing smaller, quieter, less and less connected to my essential self. I needed to find *my* balance. Not what friends and family thought of as balance, but the balance and peace that worked for my kids and me.

What was the moment that turned it all around for me, you ask? It might seem like a small thing, but it was an "aha!" moment I had with my daughter. After the divorce, I kept my married name so my kids wouldn't be judged at their Catholic school for having a different last name and coming from a "broken home". My daughter came home from school one day and said "Mom, what's your last name?" I told her "the same as yours". She said "No, it's not. You're a Feser." She was right, I was so much more a Feser than I was a married woman with her husband's last name. Weird how long it took me to realize that. All of those years, trying to protect them from what I thought was the inevitable judgement of others and the kids didn't understand or care one bit. That flipped a switch for me. I changed the importance I placed on the opinions of others. I realized in that moment that for the past seven years, I had been living to meet the expectations of others and it wasn't doing anyone any good. From then on, I chose to live my life for me and my kids and no one else. It was onward and upward from there.

I began to clear out the clutter in my life. To this day, decluttering is the first step in the wellness work I do with my clients to support them in living a happy, healthy, sexy, and wealthy life. Decluttering isn't just about getting rid of material goods, it's also about cleaning up how you think. Expectation and judgment were not serving me, so I decluttered my mindset and removed them from my thinking. I did it by deleting or removing anything in my life that I considered unhealthy. Bye-bye toxic friends, some family members, old boyfriends. Adios useless, meaningless material belongings in my home, unhealthy habits, and foods! And the list goes on.

A key to lasting balance for me, and a constant challenge, has been to let go of being serious all the time. In my younger years I was a lot of fun. In my mind, though, being a parent meant I had to set frivolous fun aside and act like a grown up, and that's what I did. So, there I was, denying my inner joy, always on duty, and perpetually afraid of judgement. I didn't allow myself any personal fun because I was afraid of looking like a bubbleheaded single mother. With the constant seriousness came an intense fear of many things I used to be fearless about. Sometimes my mama-bear instincts brought the fears. Other times, it was unnecessary anxiety that stopped me from enjoying myself. I remember one day when I was asked if I wanted to waterski. I had always loved boats, the ocean, and swimming, but that day I was terrified to get behind the boat. So strange, how wanting to appear smart, intelligent, wise, and loving snuffed all the fun out of me. What I figured out in the end, was that if I wanted to rediscover my "fun" side, I had to let go of the expectation of perfection.

Remember *George's* Mom? Well, similarly, it was by letting go of the expectation of perfection that I realized my kids and their classmates did not care one bit if their treats were store-bought and not homemade. They were eight years old, they had treats at school, they were happy.

Fully letting go of the judgement of others has taken all the strength I have. From time to time, I still think about the cruel judgement of others, but I know now that it had more to do with the scornful than the scorned. Those people had not been through a divorce, nor did they have to deal with stepfamily issues. They didn't know that I had to drag sick children to the office with me just to keep my job, or that I sometimes resorted to the food bank and the church to keep food on the table. They had no idea that we shopped at Value Village for years to ensure that we could afford a warm home and other little luxuries like pedal bikes, the movies, and vacations. You see, even today, I still have to remind myself to truly and finally *let go*.

Releasing my expectations of what my life *should* look like was also key to finally getting away from judgment. My old self would only have been happy with an idyllic nuclear family, a mother and father fulfilling their traditional roles. After many years of single parenting, I realized that my kids don't need all that. They need me. A mom who is healthy, happy, and really present for them and herself. Letting go of that picture of familial perfection has served me well. When I was married, I embraced the "housewife" mentality only to realize that it was not really me. Turns out that I love working outside the home as much as in it. I love to cook because I enjoy it not because it is expected of me. Being on my own with two small children forced me to let go of the nonsense in my life and to grow into my true and authentic self. There was no hiding from it: I *had* to live it every single day.

By letting go of expectation and perfection, I got my happy back. I have signed up for a fun dance class; I buy fun, sexy clothes and not *George's* mom's cardigans. I travel to great places, and I joke with my kids because they have a great sense of humor too. And when it feels like it might slip away, I know exactly what to do: friends, laughs, a little shopping, travel, and all the things that feed my soul.

In my wellness business, I ground all of my practices and services in the belief that fulfillment comes from being happy, healthy, sexy, and wealthy. I have learned the hard way that you cannot have those four key pillars working harmoniously together if you are consumed by chaos. You must let go of expectations to be free of the chaos and to find your best life. I recall one client in particular who struggled to let go of her story and her label. Step by step we slowly worked together so she could tell her story and release some of the shame associated with it. Although she needed to be gently pushed to work through the program, once she completed it, she felt so much lighter and empowered. She was then ready to take the next step creating her happy, healthy, sexy, and wealthy life.

Do you see now why setting yourself free of expectations is the most profound way to obtain balance? At its most essential, "balance" is stability found at the centre of acceptance. The first step to acceptance and peace is to surrender and let go of all the things that are out of your control, and you cannot control other people's expectations of you.

The act of "letting go" can be as simple as letting go of the absolutely insane way your children fold the towels. It can be letting go of the judgment from the daycare mom that says with a sneer, "isn't that nice, you let your children dress themselves." Who cares if my child wears a ninja costume to daycare? He's four years old and it's 6:30 am.

My wish for you is this: let go of the pictures of perfection you carry around in your head and any need to fulfill the expectations of others. That is how you will find the balance you seek. Trust me, I've been there and done that. I am here on the other side of the craziness to tell you that you need to define what balance means to *you* and to strive for that. Don't let anyone deter you from that goal, ignore any judgment that comes your way. Life is a one-time offer, use it well.

And finally, laugh. Some days you eat salad and go to the gym, some days you eat cupcakes and refuse to put on pants. It's called balance.

Lessons Learned:

1. Judgment has more to do with what's going on inside the person doing the judging than it has to do with you.
2. Being a responsible grown-up doesn't mean you have to stop having fun.
3. Don't let anyone else define and determine the boundaries in your life.

Mindset Tips:

1. Mindset can propel you forward or keep you stuck in a destructive pattern.
2. A self-defeating mindset is the very first thing that needs to be worked on before any other steps for a brighter future.

A-ha Moments and Self-Reflections

Note your Thoughts

_____
_____
_____
_____
_____
_____
_____
_____
_____
_____
_____
_____
_____
_____
_____
_____
_____
_____
_____
_____
_____
_____

Cheryl Hopfner

Cheryl Hopfner is a mother of five and a retired dental professional who enjoys sharing her story with women who are struggling to find balance and happiness in their lives.

She hopes that her story of going from blame, shame, deep depression, and hopelessness to a fulfilling and happy life surrounded by loving family and friends, will inspire others to do the work, go after their dreams, and discover what balance means to them. Her own conscious choice to shift her mindset, put herself first, and engage in meaningful self-care, have led her to create a positive, happy life that she could never have imagined for herself in the past.

Chapter 4:

Buried Alive by Shame and Blame –

And How I Dug my Way Out

By Cheryl Hopfner

Clomp, thump, wet black earth landing on my head, my shoulders. Darkness all around me, just a faint pre-dawn light from above. Above what? Above where? Where am I? I had a sinking feeling that I just wasn't able to shake. I was being buried alive by my life.

This was the feeling I lived with every day for four years. In that time, I frequently felt unable to breathe; the tightness in my chest and the feeling of my broken heart was terrifying. I didn't know it at the time, but I was burying myself alive. Shame and blame were the rocks and dirt of my burial. I didn't know how to stop and I sure didn't know how to dig my way out. This is the story of how I survived.

In the depths of my buried alive years, I found myself at my doctor's office waiting to find out if I had breast cancer. Sitting in that waiting room, my heart pounding, my mind wandering, my legs not able to move, I was paralyzed with fear. When I was forty-five, I watched my mother suffer through and survive breast cancer. Nobody should have to go through what I saw my mom go through, but she was a survivor and I would fight to survive like her. Just as she must have, I began thinking the unimaginable for myself and my family. What would happen to my kids if something happened to me? You see, when I was fifty-one years old, my husband left me for another woman. All of this was happening while I was trying to make critical decisions, parent as a single mother of five children (two still at home, one with Downs Syndrome), generate income, relocate our home and life, and navigate the grief of loss. My life was coming undone faster than I could rebuild it. There was no end to the pressure, stress, and fear in my life. The diagnosis came back, the biopsy was blessedly benign. Relief flooded through me momentarily, at least I would be around for my children.

Then my father passed away. Life as I knew it had, once again, been turned upside down. Loneliness, depression, fear and anxiety took over every aspect of my life. It seemed that all I ever thought about was how I was going to survive. Even though I didn't have cancer, I was fifty-one years old, alone, and terrified of what would happen next. Constant uncertainty and anxiety had taken over my life. I was an emotional and a physical wreck; a shell of my former self.

First, it was the loneliness that took over. I was lost. I didn't know how to live my life alone, nor did I want to. I would sit for hours, unaware of where the time went. All I wanted was my life back. I wanted my family back. The dream of the happy marriage was gone. I held on to a dream that maybe, just maybe, my husband would come back. I couldn't help dreaming even though I knew all too well that getting back together was not a good thing to wish for. During the marriage, I'd had to deal with mental abuse as well as alcohol and drug abuse. Heartache and regrets, and my own personal hell, were all I had now. They might have been initially triggered by the actions of others, but I was the one hanging on to them now. I was living in a grave that was being dug ever deeper by my state of mind. I piled shame and blame onto myself like I never wanted to see a day above ground again. Some days, I just locked myself in my room, lay in bed in the dark, staring at the ceiling, and ruminating. *Why me? I should have known better. What did I do to deserve such heartache?*

I was suffocating in a hole of my own digging. I was empty and dry inside, no tears left in my body. I thought my life had no meaning.

Then depression began to pound down on me, a new kind of burial. I went to some very dark places during this period. Nothing about depression was easy. It had an effect on many areas of my life, such as routines, social situations, and sleep. I was not emotionally there for anyone, especially my children who needed me most. This upheaval was happening to them as well as to me. I was feeling like a failure and sad all the time. Then there were all of the fears: would I be able to manage my new situation at my age? Could I be enough for my kids? Could I give them everything they needed emotionally? That was when I decided to see my doctor. I didn't want to be on medication, but I knew it was what I had to do, even just for a little while.

Over the next three years, life got worse. Despite the medical assistance, I continued to struggle with depression and paralyzing sadness. Then I lost my mom and was left without the two most important people in my life: my confidants and my rocks. Who would I turn to now? The grief was almost unbearable. There were times when I just wanted to be alone with my grief. I just wanted to surrender to the tears and rewind all the memories in my head. I needed time to deal with the loss and pain, to say goodbye. But I couldn't give in to grief. I had to be strong and put on a brave face for my kids. I tried so hard to hide from them how I was really feeling. I was auto piloting my way from A to B, while my mind was wandering in its own dark little world of shame and blame. What I didn't realize at the time was that all of the negative thoughts were weighing me down, adding to my stress. *Why is it that I am losing everyone I care about? What did I do that was so wrong? Why do I let people treat me this way? I know I'm not perfect but why is this happening again? Maybe it is me and I am doing something to cause this to happen again.* I was constantly looking to blame myself, even though deep in my heart, I knew none of it was my fault alone.

Incredibly, while I was married, my life looked stable, even idyllic from the outside. I was successful, and I had beautiful healthy children, and a lovely home. My husband and I had a very successful business; lots of money coming in. But it didn't take much digging for the cracks to begin to show. I remember a time when it felt like even strangers to our small town would be able to see our "dirty laundry."

I knew the relationship was over before the marriage ended. Friends would ask me why I kept trying to hold it together and I couldn't say. They didn't see the shame and blame piled up around me, blinding, and paralyzing me.

When we finally decided that it was over, the most difficult part of the process was trying to explain what was happening to my two youngest children who were still at home. Seeing what the break-up was doing to them, broke my heart. *Mommy why are you so sad? Where is Dad? Why did Daddy Leave?* They had so many questions that I didn't know how to answer in a way that they could understand. It was hard to force them to go to their dad's house knowing they didn't want to go. They would cry and cry. I had to make them understand that their dad still loved them even though he didn't live with us. Thank goodness, we lived in the same town. They knew that I was not far away and would be there if they needed me. The confusion in their faces, the sadness, the anger, as they moved back and forth between our two houses, was hard to take. I wished total stability for them, but they were home with me only three quarters of the time.

When I began to look at the hold that blame had on me, I realized it had started in my marriage. Living with blame was exhausting, exasperating, and painful. It made me feel so small, like nothing I did or said was good enough or would ever be. Not that we didn't have some good times, but we also had really dark moments that included highly toxic behaviors like mutual blaming. Blame, by its nature, provokes a defensive response. *You did this* naturally leads to *no I didn't.* I tried not to go down that path because I knew from experience that it would lead to a devastating fight. Eventually our toxic relationship broke down my trust, which was replaced by resentment and anger. I felt like an emotional punching bag. I tried so hard to show him how it made me feel but the back and forth would only make me feel worse. I kept asking myself, *Is it true? Is it my fault that I felt as I did? Am I going crazy for thinking this way?* I couldn't communicate with him anymore, I couldn't get him to see how hurt I felt and how our relationship was damaging our family. It was like I had lost all control over my emotions, my thoughts and my actions.

When my husband left our marriage to be with another woman, my inner blaming voice went crazy. *How could you not have seen it coming? How could you commit your life to someone who could do that to your family?* The crushing weight of my inner negativity felt so heavy that I no longer wanted to do anything. I would just sit and think. I just kept digging deeper and deeper into the darkness.

I remember the moment when I looked into my kids' confused faces and realized that this was not how I wanted them to grow up. They kept asking why mommy was so sad, why was I sitting so long in the dark. I wanted them to understand what I was going through but I also knew that they were not old enough. I was depressed and wrapped up in my own stuff, and it was up to me to fix the situation.

My kids are what kept me going and what helped me have the fierce resolve to claw my way out of the grave. I am not sure where I would be today without them. They helped me see that there was more to life than being married. If they had found a way to be happier despite our circumstances, then why couldn't I? They helped me see that we no longer walked on eggshells around the house. We were laughing again, smiling again, and really talking about things again. Kids are a lot more resilient than we give them credit for.

With my children's encouragement during this very stressful time, I gave myself permission to reinvent myself and change my life for the better. I began to learn that no matter how present I was in my life, there would always be highs and lows, shitty unexpected turns, and also incredibly positive ones. No matter what I did, I was never going to reach a point where everything was 100% good all of the time. So, I started to look at life in a different way. As I read in one of my many self-help books, "True happiness doesn't exist somewhere within you, it is you."

I started to see more clearly how I wanted my life to be. I wanted to be happy, I wanted to be there for my kids and show them that we were going to be just fine. I wanted them to see how much I loved them and that they were my world.

My change in attitude changed my life. It was then I decided to focus on myself, who I was and who I wanted to be. I would be grateful for my life. I would go after what made me happy. I wanted to find that confident me again. I wanted to laugh and love again. It wasn't an easy journey. It took time and energy to get to where I am today, but once I realized that I was the only one holding me back, I was finally able to make the leap. I was breathing deeply again. With the sun on my shoulders, I could finally move forward.

Now, what did I do exactly to start building a new life? Like so many women, I had always assumed that we should just know how to be happy. But in truth, I had a lot to learn about how to truly take care of myself, especially inside. It seems to me that women's stressors are different from most men's. We are constantly burning the candle at both ends and when we realize that we *can't* do it all, the stress builds up. If I wanted a more positive inner life, I needed to identify what the problems in my life were and then figure out the best way to solve them. Not as easy as it may sound. Addressing the physical and mental symptoms that I was feeling, such as low energy, insomnia, migraines, loss of appetite, and an inability to focus, was a major hurdle.

Rewiring my mindset from shame and blame to positivity and gratitude was difficult. First, I had to accept that I did not have the perfect life or the perfect marriage. I learned to only take responsibility for my own thoughts and actions. I used to feel responsible for the actions of others, but not anymore. When it came to our extended family, for example, I made sure to do everything I could to maintain healthy relationships for the sake of my children, but I no longer felt responsible for what others chose to or not to do.

To fully recover from years of feeling belittled- told that I was nothing- I put great care and attention into healing my mental health and self-worth. I had believed the negative messages I was receiving for so long that I couldn't connect to my real self and my true potential. Now, free of that outer negativity, I was not going to let it live on inside my mind. I had to fight for my life, for the person that I knew I could be.

Before really becoming aware of my mindset, I didn't realize how many deeply destructive thoughts and beliefs I was holding onto. By living from a mindset of shame and blame, I was choosing anger, resentment, and self-pity as my primary emotions. Once I realized the damage they were causing, I no longer wanted to hold on to those feelings. Mental and emotional abuse are incredibly damaging; the wounds take a very long time to heal. It takes even longer to stop believing in the lies. The impact of the abuse is virtually invisible. It causes you to question your own sanity, especially when the abuser is not even aware of the effect they are having. I lived in perpetual self-doubt; I felt like I was losing my mind. It is very painful and extremely real. Friends and family couldn't see my reality for what it was.

An essential part of rebuilding my mindset was forgiveness. It was a big step after taking the blame for so long. Forgiving myself came first and foremost, which meant that I had to work through my feelings. I struggled with that part; it was like pulling teeth out of a grumpy bear. I had to give myself a break: no more trying to be superwoman. I had to learn how to take care of myself emotionally and physically. I know it sounds like no fun at all, but, truthfully, it was extremely liberating and healing to let go of the pain. It was like being given wings and an open sky to fly in. Then, in time, I learned to forgive everyone else. I knew that letting go of all the anger and resentment would benefit me and my health, but it didn't come easy. I had to take time to heal, regroup, and re-energize. It was time to start thinking about what I wanted.

My close friends and family were always there for me, but, after a while, I felt like all I ever talked about were my problems, over and over again. I was worried about becoming *that* person that they would shy away from, so they wouldn't have to hear about my issues anymore. Then I started going to counselling. Having someone else, someone neutral, to confide in and seek advice from, was very helpful. I also read self-help book after self-help book.

My recovery process was taking so much time and energy from me, I questioned if I was getting anywhere at all. Then, when all the tears dried up and the counseling sessions felt better rather than worse, I began to dig myself out of that dark place I had been in for so long. Those walls I had built and trapped myself in, were starting to crumble. I was beginning to understand. I was learning how to deal with the changes in my life and to get some perspective on my situation, instead of coming from a place of denial and resistance. I learned that it was alright to feel sad, angry, exhausted, and confused. No matter how intense they were, those feelings were mine. I realized that I had to turn all of the negatives into positives, that it was okay if I didn't get the outcome I wanted. Embracing the situation helped me deal with the change. I was finally looking to my future and not my past. Hello sunshine!

Although still reconnecting with myself, I was learning to enjoy some of my favorite activities again, as well discovering new ones. I stopped hiding inside my house, as I had done for years. I began to go out, to make new friends, and to have fun. I let people into my life. I let myself be known and seen and loved. I developed a more positive mindset. I learned that acceptance was very healing for me, that things were never going to be the same again, and that I could move on.

After a year of shoveling myself out from under the shame and blame, I began noticing positive shifts in my life. Where my thoughts before were dark, brooding, and inescapable, they were now positive and full of hope. Where I used to feel numb inside, I started to tingle with vitality and openness. It felt great and I wanted more. I was healing.

Nobody teaches us how to allow ourselves to feel our emotions healthily, yet we need emotions to heal. From an early age, I was taught to shut down and hide my feelings. I was somehow weak if allowed my true feelings to show. As I healed, I realized that I wasn't even slightly the crazy, useless person I had felt I was during my marriage. I am a good person, kindhearted to a fault sometimes. I started to laugh again.

One day, several months into my new shame-free life, I was at home with the kids and my youngest daughter said, "Mommy it's good to see you smile." I hugged her and cried tears of happiness because I could feel how right she was, how much I had changed. I knew then that I was beginning to make lasting positive changes. To keep my life going in that positive direction, I developed the daily habit of doing two or three positive things that made me happy. Small but powerful things like having a peaceful coffee in the morning before the kids woke up or telling my kids how wonderful they are to me and how much I love them. By then it felt incredible to remember a time when I didn't even have enough positive energy to do that! As I got further and further from the grave, I learned to celebrate tiny victories. I also realized that having a positive attitude doesn't mean that I am never in a bad mood. Instead I came to understand that stress and bad moods are just a part of life. It is normal to worry and feel vulnerable sometimes.

Despite everything I went through, I am now the happiest I have ever been. My children are happy, and I am present in my own life. Our life is good again.

I know now that all of my hard work has been worth it because I am finally able to take charge of my thoughts and stories and it can be the same for you. No matter how much the world tries to hold you back, always continue forward with the belief that anything is possible. Believing that you can do it is essential for achieving success. If you believe, you will always find a way to overcome the obstacles that you encounter. After all, struggle is how we identify and develop our strengths. If five years ago I had been asked if I thought I could change my life for the better, I would have said no. Now I know it is totally possible. If you want to change your life, you just have to take that first step. It will be the biggest ever but well worth it. You *can* do it.

"I forgive myself

For having believed for so long,

That I was never good enough

To have, get & be

What I wanted."

Ceanne DeRohan

I would not have necessarily chosen the experiences or the pain I went through, but they have shaped me into the person I am today.

That person is worthy and loveable.

Lessons Learned:

1. A healthy, happy life requires regular, positive, self-care.
2. Giving up is *not* an option, you have to fight for who you want to be and the life you want to have.
3. You have the power. Even if it seems scary to think that no one can save you but you, it also means that you hold the power within you to create the life you want.
4. It is up to each and every one of us to take that first step toward healing. It is the hardest, but also the most rewarding. Once you take it, there will be no going back.

Mindset Tips:

1. Lose the fear of being yourself. Don't be afraid of defining your own identity, regardless of what others may want or say.
2. Love who you are. Know that you are a valuable human being regardless of whatever negative messaging you have internalized until now.
3. Choose change and stay open to the possibilities.

A-ha Moments and Self-Reflections

Note your Thoughts

_____

_____

_____

_____

_____

_____

_____

_____

_____

_____

_____

_____

_____

_____

_____

_____

_____

_____

_____

_____

_____

Susannah Juteau

Susannah Juteau, M.Sc., RD, is a registered dietitian who specializes in headache nutrition. She has a bachelor's degree in Neuroscience and a master's in Nutrition and Dietetics from McGill University.

Somewhat ironically, her study of the brain seems to have foreshadowed her own health challenges, which resulted in a ten-hour brain surgery to remove a benign tumour the size of a ping pong ball. Post-surgery, she struggled for years with her mindset, energy levels, and constant headaches.

Finally, after resigning from her job and moving to California, she began experimenting with therapeutic fasting. Sixteen weeks in, she was off her headache meds completely, back to her usual body weight, and energized like never before.

Today, she teaches others how to overcome their migraines naturally.

Connect with Susannah:
www.headachenutritionist.com
https://www.instagram.com/headachenutritionist/
https://www.facebook.com/headachenutritionist

Chapter 5:

When Life Gives You Lemons

By Susannah Juteau

It's funny how a phone call that should have been the worst news of my life ended up being a huge relief. After I got the phone call, I actually felt giddy. Immediately, I texted my Dad: "Supposedly I have a brain tumour. At least it's not all in my head!"

The headaches had started a few days after I hit my head while skiing with friends. I spent the next two months going back and forth to the doctor. I'd tell them I couldn't function at work anymore, that I had constant headaches, and that they were getting worse. They'd do the typical concussion psychological evaluation, which I'd always ace, and then tell me to rest and return to work whenever I felt comfortable.

As a kid, I had numerous health issues: a dog bite on my left cheek and my ear bitten off, a rare bone disorder that took years to diagnose, and more stiches than any other kid I knew. I was used to pretending that pain didn't faze me, so I could be just like all the other kids and avoid going back to the hospital. I had learned how to mask my symptoms and hold completely engaged conversations regardless of how I felt. Consequently, I wasn't used to expressing how I really felt; I had a hard time describing my pain properly and convincing the doctors that the headaches were magnifying each day and this wasn't a concussion. The turmoil inside my head was telling me that something more serious was going on.

Eventually, I had to be my own advocate and insist on an MRI. That's when they found it, a brain tumour the size of a ping pong ball. I was relieved that my inability to function could be explained, but, soon after my diagnosis, I began to suffer emotionally because I was afraid of losing everything.

I was afraid of losing the amazing partnership I had with my boyfriend Mark. He had moved into my apartment a couple of weeks after the ski trip. A move, which, I guess, came as a surprise to my family because my dad got a speeding ticket minutes after I told him that Mark was moving in. I was determined not to play the victim or let my health issues mess up our relationship, so I hid the wincing, never complained about the pain, and refused to share how I was really feeling with anyone.

I was also afraid of losing the job that I had worked so hard to get and afraid of losing cherished friends. But, more than anything, I was afraid of never returning to the woman I had been before the tumour started taking bits and pieces of me away.

I usually have an almost "faniac" fascination with scientific literature, but in this case, I stayed away from all research related to my tumour. All I knew was that it was an acoustic neuroma pushing on my brainstem that required an immediate, life-saving surgery. My parents were my angels and my advocates: they came prepared for every doctor's appointment with a list of questions, they read up on the procedures, analyzed multiple research articles and, more than anything, kept me distracted. They're both very clever, so I'm sure they were well aware that the daily outings, lunches, and activities were also vital for keeping me in the right state of mind going into surgery.

Two days before my operation, Mark proposed. It didn't matter to him that my body was a lemon. He loved every piece of me and was willing to be there through the struggles no matter what. Celebrating our engagement was a great distraction for what was to come.

The night before my procedure, we lay clutching each other tightly, tears streaming down our faces. "You have to move on if my personality changes at all or if my health becomes a burden," I sobbed.

The story of Phineas Gage filled my thoughts and fueled my fear that my behaviour would change dramatically. Mark didn't deserve a lifetime of hardship on my account.

What was supposed to be a four-hour surgery ended up lasting nine and a half hours. My parents and Mark sat in silence in the waiting room, anxiously awaiting news the entire time.

I was determined to show everyone that I would be the fastest healer they had ever seen. When friends came to visit the hospital, I would immediately turn to my old coping mechanisms and pretend that I wasn't in any pain. I'd laugh, try to walk down the hall, ask questions about what was going on in their lives, reminisce, and wave off any concern for how my healing process was going.

Any visit longer than twenty minutes was too much for my brain to handle, but rather than say that I needed to cut our visit short, I would let them stay as long as they liked and then suffer in silence for hours afterward. All just to get a "gold star" for being the picture of strength, resilience, and health.

My need to prove myself even crossed over into my physiotherapy sessions.

A week after my surgery, on my first day back home, a facial physiotherapist came to work the muscles on the left side of my face, which had been paralyzed due to the complicated nature of the procedure. She spent a half hour explaining the neuronal muscular processes behind my paralysis. I sat and listened, even though my brain couldn't handle that level of concentration. I figured that, having worked with post-brain-surgery patients, she must know how much interaction her clients could tolerate, so I tried to step it up and do what I was supposed to do.

I began to break into a heavy sweat and started to feel sick. My resolve was strong; I still didn't say anything. Luckily, my wonderful sister was helping me out that day. She is an ICU nurse. She noticed I wasn't well and made me lie down, then shuttled the physiotherapist out so I could rest.

Along with the physical demands of my recovery, I was in so much pain that I thought my brain would explode. Honestly, sometimes I wished it would because then at least the pain would go away. My mental health suffered and my emotional turmoil grew.

I felt angry, hurt, and disappointed by friends and family who didn't visit right away. I also felt disappointed by people who visited but then never followed up. It seemed that they had done "their duty" and then moved on. I blamed others for not caring. Thoughts like, *If people aren't there for you when you have brain surgery then when will they be?* and, *Why have friends at all?* crept into my consciousness.

And yet, I never once shared how I was feeling or reached out to those I hoped would visit. Whenever I was asked how I was doing, I would say, "Great! I'll be back to work in no time. Did you know I managed to walk all the way down the street and back and I stayed awake for a few hours in a row? Hooray!" Putting on this show for everyone was exhausting, but it felt like a state of being, rather than something I could control

One benefit of having had so many health issues as a kid is that my mom learned how to read me like a book. She took over a month off work and visited me every day. My sister, knowing I wouldn't remember a lot of it, had the idea of encouraging visitors to write well-wishes and messages of strength and hope in a journal so that I'd have something to look back on.

My mom spent each day sitting silently next to me, writing in the journal while I slept on the couch. As I was unable to handle stimulation of any kind, she had no expectation that I would engage with her or pretend that I was feeling better than I did. She was my pillar of strength and my gratitude is hard to articulate or put in writing. In fact, it is unlikely that I will ever fully grasp the extent of her contribution to my recovery.

During this period, Mark was completing a work internship and wasn't able to take any time off. When he got home at night, my mom would go "off-duty." Though Mark may not have understood, as my mother did, the extent to which I internalized pain, he was just as patient as she was. Typically, he's quite talkative, but he knew I wouldn't be able to handle it, so we spent many evenings cuddled on the couch, the only chatter coming from the thoughts in our head.

After five months, I was able to stay awake for longer stretches of time and became determined to return to work. As a community dietitian, I loved connecting with people and helping them with their health journey. Daily physical activity was my main means of self-care, and, miraculously, was one of the only ways my headaches would subside.

My disability health insurance provider, who was still debating whether or not to pay out my claim, decided that if I could do exercise, I could go back to work. I agreed. I wanted to win the non-existent prize for healing and returning to work in record time.

As it turns out though, my return to work was the absolute hardest part of my recovery in every way: physically, mentally, and emotionally.

My façade wasn't sustainable. I would give my all at work only to deliver a mediocre performance, then I'd struggle to walk home only to crash as soon as I came through the door. Working at my previous level of ability, was next to impossible. Looking back, I've realized my tumour and resulting surgery, had triggered the migraine pathway. Once those mechanisms are in full-force, it is extremely difficult to get headaches under control.

Unfortunately, in situations such as these, it is often the insurance company that makes the decisions. My insurance pushed forward with a return-to-work plan that I was required to follow. My hours quickly increased until, within six weeks, I was back to full-time hours with a full-time schedule. It was as if I had never left. But I was not confident enough, or mentally healthy enough, to be my own advocate.

For months, I just went through the motions, barely coping. I wasn't the best dietitian I could be. Somehow, no one noticed. I wasn't the best friend I could be, either. Again, no one noticed. Or, if they did, they didn't say anything. I most certainly wasn't the best fiancée I could be. I'm sure Mark noticed, but luckily, he was very understanding and never complained.

Mark and I spent our honeymoon in Vietnam and Cambodia, a whole month during which my headaches responded better to medication than they ever had before. Without the stress of work and having to perform at previous levels, I started to feel in control of my head again. But when the vacation ended, my headaches and dizziness returned with a vengeance and I had to take time off again.

All-in-all, it took a couple of years of trial and error with many visits to neurologists, different types of medications, a focus on my nutrition and trying to assess what my new stress tolerance was, before I finally got to a place where my headaches could be largely controlled.

On the day of my second child Jasmine's birth, yet another phone call would change the course of my life. Mark got an offer to work at Google. We spent two months going back and forth in our minds, trying to decide whether he should take the job or not. It meant packing up our life and moving west, clear across the continent to California.

Although it was the best choice for Mark's career, we weren't sure it was the best decision for our family. Both sets of grandparents and most of our friends lived close by in Ottawa, I enjoyed my job serving the community I had grown to love, and we knew it would be five times more expensive to live in Silicon Valley; we would barely be able to make ends meet.

Jasmine was two months old when we moved.

Luckily, I still got my full year of maternity leave; so, I spent those early months enjoying quality time with my girls, exploring our new city, and making some wonderful new friends. We were also fortunate to have my brother and his wife living in the same city, which allowed us to still spend a lot of time with family.

My life felt balanced in many ways, but there were two very important areas I still needed to work on. First, I still had to take headache medication daily and I didn't want to be on meds for the rest of my life. I didn't want to suffer because I forgot to take a pill at night or because I didn't exercise that day. Just like when I was a kid, I wanted to fit in and be "normal".

Second, in the five years since my surgery, my energy levels had plummeted, and I had gained a lot of weight for my body. I had all kinds of excuses: it was the surgery, the medications, the pregnancies, the constant hunger that came with breastfeeding. All true, but that didn't make me feel any better. The fact is that I was eating all of the time.

Sure, it was healthy food, but eating every three to four hours was not serving me very well. I *always* felt hungry. The reality is that I'm not sure I knew what hunger was anymore. My body felt hungry based on external cues, not true hunger. I often felt ashamed when I told people what my profession was. I was afraid that they would judge me, or worse, not find my information credible since I couldn't apply it to my own life.

My nine-to-five job at the Community Health Centre in Ontario had kept me so busy with all of the programs I was running, I had never been able to dig into the emerging research, but people kept asking about intermittent fasting. Now that I was on "mat leave," I had the time, so I spent months pouring over the literature. Although the research was in its early stages, there was quite a bit of compelling evidence arguing *for* fasting to improve gut health, longevity, metabolism, reverse autoimmune disorders and most importantly for me: brain health. Compelling enough for me to try it for myself.

I had come across some anecdotal evidence of people curing their migraines with regular fasting, which gave me hope. For the first month, I followed the 16:8 protocol, fasting for sixteen hours a day and eating during the remaining eight-hour window. It was fairly easy to follow, but my headaches didn't improve.

After a month, I realized that a longer, more therapeutic, fasting interval might be more beneficial because it meant that I would be in the state of ketosis and autophagy for longer periods. Ketosis is a metabolic state where the body burns stored fat for energy rather than glucose, which is advantageous for the brain. Autophagy is where the body cleans out old damaged cells and toxins to promote new cell growth and healthy neurons. I had also just finished watching Michael Mosley's "Eat, Fast and Live Longer" BBC documentary and read his book where he encourages the 5:2 protocol. So, I started fasting for twenty-four-hour periods on Mondays and Thursdays.

I found the first two weeks difficult, as I got used to my new ketosis-inducing eating pattern. After that, however, I found the fasting to be quite flexible, manageable, and, dare I say, easy. I would stop eating after supper on Sunday and start eating again at supper on Monday. As a result, I never missed a meal with my girls, which was important because I wanted them to grow up with healthy eating habits, and I wanted to prioritize eating together as a family.

Within four weeks, I was able to cut my headache medication in half. By eight weeks, I was off the medication completely. My weight returned to normal and I was amazed at the energy I felt. My mental health also improved because I was finally regaining balance and normalcy in my life.

Today, my relationship with Mark has never been better. He stuck with me through my tough recovery, stood by me as I adjusted to hearing loss and facial paralysis, and encouraged me to focus on the positive when my mind was in its deepest turmoil. All along, he never saw a lemon but rather someone with resolve and resilience. With his support and patience, we came through this life challenge, our bond not only intact but stronger than it would have been otherwise. An experience we will pass on to our girls.

My friendships have also flourished, now that I am able to connect on a deeper level. I have become calmer, more understanding, and less reactive. I am not sure of the exact cause for these positive changes in my life. Was it that the tumour had been (mostly) removed? Was it that my daily headaches were finally under control? Was it the result of the personal growth that came with my recovery? Or was it simply that we were all reminded that life is short?

If nothing else, going through hardship taught me to advocate for myself. Now, I get to step into my power and educate women on the benefits of overthrowing the traditional eating paradigm for controlling their migraines. That is so *powerful*. Sharing my knowledge and my experience is what makes me a terrific dietitian, regardless of whether I have a "perfect smile" or not.

I never imagined that I would actually be *thankful* for a brain tumour, but fighting to regain my mental, physical, and emotional health has made me realize how strong and resilient I truly am. Now, I know: there's *nothing* I can't handle.

Lessons Learned:

1. Figure out what values are important to you and live by them. I am now a free, open, joyful woman. You'd better believe that I will work every single day to stay that way so that I can make my parents proud and serve as a great model for my girls.
2. Be honest and don't expect people to guess what you are thinking. To avoid being overwhelmed and maintain balance in your life, say what you want and ask for what you need. Don't be a lone wolf.
3. Be open to learning new things. If I hadn't been open to experimenting with fasting, I would probably still be struggling — being headache-free and regaining my energy are only two of many ways that IF has restored balance in my life.

Mindset Tips:

1. Don't focus on balance, instead, focus on your purpose *in this moment*. We spend so much time worrying about either the past or the future that we forget what it means to be fully present.
2. Be your own best advocate and let go of the "people pleasing." Stick up for yourself, listen to your gut.
3. Share your feelings and be vulnerable; it will bring you closer to those you love.
4. Be aware of your limitations. If I had been honest with myself I would have set boundaries that were consistent with my values and I could have avoided a lot of emotional turmoil.
5. You own your story, it's up to you how it is written.

A-ha Moments and Self-Reflections

Note your Thoughts

_____

_____

_____

_____

_____

_____

_____

_____

_____

_____

_____

_____

_____

_____

_____

_____

_____

_____

_____

_____

_____

Cindy Klamn-Conway

Cindy Klamn-Conway was born and raised in Edmonton, Alberta by her father, Hank Klamn. Cindy had a very close relationship with her father that left lasting imprints on her heart. When she was thirty-five years old, Cindy and her husband packed up and moved to Calgary where they raised their three beautiful children.

In her life, Cindy has faced many challenges, but never allowed fear to knock her down. She thrives on her strength and positivity to turn all situations into life lessons. She is a natural born Intuitive Spiritual Guide/Medium who chooses to use her gift to bring happiness and peace into the lives of others who may need support or answers in the darkest times of their lives. She brings a unique blend of passion, honesty, and equality that she spreads throughout her community and family. She embraces people without judgment, she accepts them as they are, and comes to them from a place of authenticity.

Connect with Cindy:
https://www.facebook.com/AbovetheCloudsWithCindy/

Chapter 6:

The Power of Positive Thinking

By Cindy Klamn-Conway

My dad, who belonged to Alcoholics Anonymous off and on through the years, taught me so much about taking responsibility for my life. He was a man of few words, but his actions demonstrated his convictions. He kept the vows made to my mother, even after she passed away – *My dad's word meant something to him.*

My dad believed there was always a solution, no matter what the circumstances. If he couldn't find one, he would improvise. When he was sober, people would still offer him a drink, so his solution was to always have an alcohol-free drink in his hand. I thought that was so clever. —*My dad was skilled at figuring things out.*

My dad and I would go to his meetings and I would support him in any way I could. I would listen as they said the Serenity Prayer. As a child I did not fully understand its meaning. I thought it was only for alcoholics, until I really read it, listened carefully to the words, and actually heard and understood it—*My dad's life was defined by these words:*

God, grant me the serenity to accept the things I cannot change,

Courage to change the things I can,

And wisdom to know the difference.

The first line, "accept the things I cannot change" helped me to understand that I do not have control over everything that happens around me, which was not easy because I believe that change *is always* possible. But now I know when to let go, and I am okay with it.

I have always believed in the power of positive thinking, the power to find love in all things, and that there is a reason for everything. I have always firmly believed that *I* am the *agent of change* in my life. I may not control everything, but I decide what I want, and I decide what changes I need to make in order to achieve that outcome. What I decide to change is not dependent on the opinions of others. The second line in the Serenity Prayer, "Courage to change things I can," reminds me that it often takes courage to effect change and that change is a choice. I can choose whether to benefit others or only myself, to discover a new perspective, to explore a new way of thinking, to find a new path forward. When I put my mind to it, if I choose, my life can always change for better.

The last line of this prayer "the wisdom to know the difference," is very empowering for me. I understand it to mean that not only do I not control everything, but it is up to me to recognize *what* changes I *should* make. Even if I believe that I can change *anything* that is within my control, I can't change *everything*. Change takes time and focus. It is important to prioritize and choose wisely.

To this day, the Serenity Prayer still guides me in my daily life.

I thought my life was going according to plan. I was happily married to my husband, Bruce, and together we brought three fabulous children into this world. We had decided that I would stay home with the kids. In addition to raising our three children, I ended up running a day home, another small business on the side, and, on top of it all, we had decided to home school. There were many long, exhausting days, but it was worth the effort as this would allow us to instil our morals and values in our children.

When the kids were older, we decided that I would go back to work and the money I made would be used for investments, travel, and university. I felt like I had laced up my shoes and was ready to play! I had a plan. I was feeling good about getting a job and contributing financially to our family. Then, *life happened*.

Well, as they say, "life happens, while you're planning it."

I was driving on a beautiful sunny day, when I was forced to stop because of an accident ahead. Unfortunately, the driver behind me was not paying attention and hit me. Next thing I knew, I was in a five-car pileup, my forehead hit the steering wheel, my body twisted and froze, and, when it was over, my head was almost resting on my left shoulder.

That was the start of a very long nightmare that would go on for years. In those few seconds, not only had the left side of my body seized up, leaving me wracked with pain and in constant discomfort, I also suffered significant brain damage, which affected my motor control as well as my memory. I was shattered.

I was constantly confused. I had forgotten how to complete the most basic tasks. I had to relearn everything. Activities I used to take for granted, like making coffee in the morning, were now completely foreign concepts to me. Counting, measuring, or anything that required math, was nearly impossible. And, to make things worse, my short-term memory was also a mess. I would go up to people who looked familiar and ask them if they knew me.

A quick trip to the grocery store would last for hours. Navigating around to get items on my grocery list was very confusing. I could read that I needed butter but then I would think, "*What does that mean? Where do I get butter when I am by the apples?*" And, I was always losing my grocery cart. At first, it was humiliating to ask strangers for help with finding things, but I drummed up the courage anyway. People were very helpful, but when I walked away, I would forget what they had said and where they had told me to go. Sometimes I felt like sitting down and crying in the middle of the store. *How could something as easy as grocery shopping be so hard?*

I carried around a book with a daily to-do list of items written by my kids, my husband, or me. If something wasn't on my list, I would simply forget to do it that day (even something as simple as brushing my teeth.) I also had to mark everything on a calendar. If the calendar didn't match my list, I would get confused about what to do that day. I would forget appointments, events, and everyday responsibilities. My family often joked that I was like Drew Barrymore's character in *50 First Dates*. We'd watch a video and the next night I'd pick it up and say, "Let's watch this movie." When they told me, we had already watched it together, I could feel their frustration. I felt like a burden.

My children were between eleven and fifteen years old, so during the tough teenage years when they needed me the most to guide them, lead them, and give them morals and values, I wasn't there for them. Bruce pressured them to "help Mom out," but they were resistant at times, understandably so. They should have been out riding their bikes and being kids instead of having to care for me. I couldn't cook or clean or take care of my most basic needs; the responsibility fell to them. The stress led to arguments between them, and I could tell that they were really angry with me. Without me at the helm, our household was a zoo. I felt like a failure as a mother.

There were times when I would get really down, especially when the pain was too much to handle. I was spending more time flat on my back than anything else. It was so depressing, I felt like I was just existing. This wasn't the life I wanted, nor was it the life I had "planned". It made me feel like killing myself, I thought I was such a burden on my husband and family that they would be better off without me. It saddens me now when I think back on it, but I made a plan to end it all. I wasn't going be confined to a wheelchair or make my children bear the responsibility of having to put me in a home.

My husband and I went through quite a few marriage counsellors. He was frustrated that I couldn't do things. He didn't get that the effort alone, would make me pass out or throw up from the pain. At times, he would get upset and tell me how hard he was working. He just didn't understand why I couldn't function normally. I stopped asking. I would literally crawl up the stairs or lie on the floor next to my bed rather than ask him for help. I felt so alone.

And what about the additional financial strain on my family? Well, there were times that I really felt that I had no option but to make my final exit. Thankfully, my vows still meant something to me, and my dad had taught me that my word was my bond, that I wasn't allowed to give up.

I decided that I wasn't going to let my condition beat me. By the grace of God, my husband and I got through it.

Going to doctor, and specialists' appointments three to five times a week was exhausting, but I was willing to try anything to get better. Nevertheless, my life seemed like an endless stream of medical appointments. I was on that medical rollercoaster for over seven years: hoping that the next appointment would provide a solution and then feeling let down when it didn't. I had put together what I thought was a medical team that would support my journey to better health. It consisted of an acupuncturist, massage therapist, chiropractor, a team of doctors at the Pain Management Clinic, and countless other specialists. I had so much faith in them. I really believed that they would help me get my health back. Get my *life* back.

I was prescribed Oxycontin, but it didn't even begin to touch my pain. I told my doctors that I didn't want to continue on the medication because it wasn't giving me any relief. Their solution was, "We'll keep upping your dose." They knew that I was driving because they had asked me how I was getting to and from my appointments. At that time, I relied heavily on their advice, and assumed that if my driving was an issue, they would tell me, especially since they knew I had children in the car. I had so much trust in them that I believed that

I could drive, although I now realize that I was so heavily medicated, I should never have been behind the wheel. According to the doctors who helped me detox years later, I was taking the equivalent of 1000mg of heroin a day.

As the years went by, I felt caught in a vicious circle. Going to the doctor would cause me pain, then I would have to sleep because I was exhausted from the appointment, but I would be in too much pain to sleep, so they would increase my dosage. I didn't know how medicated I actually was, I just knew the drugs didn't work. My daughter once described me as, "a drug addict who takes medication and sleeps a lot." Although I was following doctor's orders, I can't disagree with her.

I talked to my doctors for months about coming off the drugs they had prescribed. Unfortunately, they wouldn't listen to me, and, because I was so medicated, I continued to follow their advice.

I was often told that my lack of acceptance was at the root of my pain. Not only was my resistance creating a mental block, but my refusal to use a walker or a wheelchair was making my pain worse. Different doctors pressured me to get into a wheelchair because, they argued, it would greatly reduce my pain. My response was, "No! You have got the wrong person!" I had also spent over $64,000 on chiropractors, massage therapists, and acupuncture treatments, but their effects were only temporary.

I knew I couldn't follow the doctors' advice: I couldn't give up. Maybe that pressure was what I needed to light a fire in me. I realized that my so-called "team" of professionals was no longer invested in my physical and mental health. If I wanted to get better, I would have to do it myself.

I went to my doctor with my decision to get off of the pain medication she had prescribed. She advised me against stopping cold-turkey and she said that I needed to be weaned from the drugs under medical supervision. So, I checked into the hospital for two weeks. The first day, I said I wanted to cut my meds by half, but the doctor wanted me to taper off more gradually to avoid the discomfort of withdrawal.

After we argued about it, I chose to cut down by fifty percent anyway, and, as it turns out, I suffered no withdrawal. I had put the power of positive thinking to work. I had believed I would not experience any withdrawal symptoms and I didn't.

I experienced an enormous shift in my mind and body after I came off the medications. It felt like my body was being properly realigned, so that my brain could now send messages to the right places. It was an empowering feeling. Then my husband came home with a gift.

His boss had attended a silent auction and won a "Chi Treatment." She didn't think she would use it and gave it to me. With a positive attitude, I jumped on the opportunity to try something new.

The Serenity Prayer and what my dad had taught me about personal responsibility and improvisation, gave me the strength to make the leap and go in a different direction. I was on a new path, a path to health, not a wheelchair. I chose to have "the courage to change the things I can." I didn't even look up what the treatment included or even what a Chi Treatment *was*. I believed that if I had an open, positive mind, it would work.

It was not a good day for me. I was in severe pain. In fact, I had to use my arms to pick up my legs to get in the car. I cried in pain all the way to the appointment. When I arrived, I was given a full description of the machines I was going to use. This included a chi machine, E-power machine, far infrared pad, and far infrared dome.

My understanding was that the chi machine would relax my muscles, relieve tension, release toxin build-up, induce alpha wave relaxation in my brain, and, when positioned correctly, realign my spine, allowing oxygen to flow freely through my system. The E-power machine would create a balanced electrical field in my body, promote higher metabolism, and help build immunity. The infrared pads would heat my body to improve circulation and, I believe, help remove toxins from my system as well. I was told that sixty percent of the effectiveness of the treatment came after the chi machine was turned off and that if I lay still afterward, I would experience a "chi rush".

As a non-invasive, non-medicated approach, the treatment resonated with me - *this was getting better every minute!* I lay down with my ankles in the chi machine, the pad under me, and the dome over me. I remained there for thirty minutes. Then the chi rush hit me at the end. It was like my body was full of champagne bubbles. It was cool but strange at the same time.

After my treatment, I didn't feel much of a difference, initially. Then, I went out to my car and jumped in. *I jumped in!* Something I had not been able to do for years. I remember sitting there, crying and crying. I could not believe what had just happened. It had only taken one hour, *what the heck?* I arrived home with a new lease on life, *I had found the secret to healing myself.*

I talked to Bruce and the kids, and we decided to purchase the machines for my own use. Thankfully the government recognizes them as medical equipment, so the expense was a tax write-off. I started using the machines once a day for thirty minutes, then I moved to twice a day. The difference in my body was miraculous. I was taking my life back, literally one day at a time. Still, I had good days and bad days. When the pain was bad, it was unbearable. But, little by little, there were more good days than bad.

I started to work on my memory as well. I enlisted the help of my children to help me relearn basic skills I had lost - *nothing like teaching Mom how to color inside the line*s. They would work daily with me. I know it was frustrating for them, but we tried to get through it with a lot of humor. I could finally see some light at the end of the tunnel.

During this period, I often volunteered at the bingo sessions run by my son's hockey team. My friends would help me navigate the volunteering duties by giving me tasks I could manage. I couldn't handle the money at first because I still wasn't good with math, but they would challenge me in other ways, such as giving out bonanza cards, for example, or bringing change to "the third person at the third table." The bingo players would also help me count, "I need two of those." They would make good natured jokes about how many times I would have to come back because I kept forgetting what I was supposed to do. It was all in fun and they were very supportive. Having smiling faces all around me was such an uplifting experience. *Now, I have a team*! I thought.

That summer, I decided to buy myself a bike to celebrate my successes. I started off small by staying in the cul-de-sac. Then I gradually went for longer and longer rides. The freedom that came with every triumphant push of the pedal, was so liberating. I was overcome with a sense of vindication. I had taken my healing into my own hands and that decision had made all the difference. The medical professionals might not have believed in me, but I had had the wisdom to know what I could change and the courage to do it.

That same summer, two good friends of mine and I went camping in Canmore, Alberta. We rode our bikes on the Rocky Mountain Legacy Trail and went from Canmore to Banff and back in a single day. It was one of the most exhilarating moments of my life. I was so proud of myself for what I had accomplished. Today, I am grateful that I had the wisdom to know what I could change, I was in control of my health and my life. The power of positive thinking, and my sheer stubbornness, brought me to this moment.

My healing now comes from sharing my truth. I have found my calling as a healer and coach, which has not only helped to create the lifestyle my husband and I wanted for our family, but has also helped fulfil my desire to help others. I use chi treatments and my gift as a medium to help clients find their way out of the dark. I tell people about my adventures through the medical system and the healing I found by trusting my intuition, and when they use my equipment, it is like an energy boomerang – the energy I am putting into others comes back to heal me too. It is a very positive experience for everyone.

Although my journey was not always easy as a parent, my bond with my children has grown stronger every year. I now have three successful, responsible, amazing adults who love and respect their mom as a positive model of resilience: they saw me go from prone and depressed, to up and out of the door, energized! Like me, they grew up living by the concepts of the *Serenity Prayer* and they have met their own obstacles with immense courage and wisdom. I couldn't be more proud.

Recently, they planned a surprise for our thirtieth wedding anniversary. We received an invitation to show up in Banff wearing black and white, so we did. It turns out that our kids had arranged a special ceremony for us to renew our vows.

Everything I had worked for, everything I had done to raise these beautiful human beings, came together in that moment. It was an extraordinary and unforgettable event for our entire family.

I know my dad would be so proud of me. I had the strength to take responsibility for my life and I fought for my health, my marriage, and my family. When the medical system was failing me, I improvised. I had the courage to challenge the future they had decided was mine, and I had the wisdom to know that the power to change was in my hands. Although I still have healing to do, I know I am making a difference in this world and I finally feel like my mind, body, and soul are aligned.

Lessons Learned:

1. Your mind is stronger than you think. Focus on what you need, put your energy towards making the change you want. I did, and it gave me the strength to heal myself.
2. Only you have the power to decide what is in your control and what you can change. I respected my doctors, but I never gave up on the belief that my body would continue to improve, even when they did.
3. Sometimes it is up to you to find the solution. When conventional therapy didn't work, and my doctors had given up on me, I went in search of options. I found my own path to healing.

Mindset Tips:

1. Focus your efforts on alignment. When my mind, body, and soul were finally aligned, I found the ultimate balance.
2. Never give up on yourself, you will be amazed at the results when you trust yourself and persevere.
3. Keep an open mind and be willing to try something new. When conventional Western Medicine failed me, I decided to try another route.

A-ha Moments and Self-Reflections

Note your Thoughts

_____

_____

_____

_____

_____

_____

_____

_____

_____

_____

_____

_____

_____

_____

_____

_____

_____

_____

_____

_____

_____

Sarah Konelsky

Sarah Konelsky, a self-proclaimed prairie girl with an island heart, lives in Calgary, Alberta. Married to her best friend and high-school sweetheart, together they have raised two beautiful souls.

Traveling and writing inspire Sarah to wander the globe, seeking experiences that engage her spirit in meaningful connection and personal growth. Her passion for Hawaiiana led to her becoming haumāna (a student) of the Aloha Music Camp, a project of the Mohala Hou Foundation "dedicated to promoting the (worldwide) teaching and sharing of Hawaiian music, dance, language and culture". Her passion for pursuing personal excellence stems from creating the life she desires through the coaching and mentoring of Erin Skye Kelly and Associates, including her incredible Achievement Club team.

In October 2018, Sarah was granted the gift of caring for and bearing witness to the final phase of her mother's journey as her soul gently transitioned from a single life force to one of universal energy.

Connect with Sarah:
kaimana-essentials@shaw.ca

Chapter 7:

Just Ask

by Sarah Konelsky

Kupu aʻe, kupu lā

Kupu i ka Leokani

Kupu i ka ua Waiʻākōlea ē.

E Kupu au.

The preceding chant was composed in 2017 by my Hawaiian chant class instructor, Kumu Liko Puha. He is one of several mentors who come together on a yearly basis to generously share their time and expertise with those who wish to delve deeper into Hawaiian culture. The essence of this chant is encouragement and affirmation to metaphorically grow like the tender shoots of a little forest fern. Strengthen your spirit through the sound of your voice blended with the eternal echo of those whose wisdom inspires you (the wind) and through the absorption of the life-giving waters that nourish your body and soul (the rain). It is one among several compositions I have learned over the years that have encouraged me to grow, especially during difficult times.

Sprout, grow

Grow in the Leokani wind

Grow in the Waiʻākōlea rain

I will grow.

Those who know me recognize that I am all about the story: talking, writing, reading, and living the story is what connects me to myself and those around me. From as far back as I can remember I've loved being a storyteller, whether playing with my imaginary friends as a little girl, being the narrator of the school play, or documenting the latest family travel adventure. I am definitely more comfortable behind the pen writing *about* my subject than *being* the subject. For me, writing has become an outlet to express how I feel while attempting to make sense of the world around me and my small part in it.

Most of the time, I share upbeat, lighthearted stories illustrated by picturesque snapshots. This story, however, is different. It is more of a love story, one that contains lessons I have learned from experiencing loss, processing grief, and trying to maintain a sense of equilibrium in the midst of chaos. While I don't identify with any specific organized religion, I do walk this Earth with an unwavering sense of spirituality—a connection with someone or something "out there" that is ready, willing, and able to provide guidance. By asking for help, often in non-conventional ways, I have learned to cope and restore my sense of balance.

Some life lessons come fast and furious while others emerge over time, building momentum until their truth can no longer be denied. The latter is how I came to the heart-wrenching conclusion that my mom's occasional forgetfulness was not "part of the aging process," as she put it, but an early indication of dementia. After her diagnosis in 2008, I struggled to find my footing for several years, until I sought help. Through the compassionate guidance and loving support of several phenomenal coaches, I began learning how to set personal goals, recognize and shift stagnant energy levels, be intentional with my time and resources, share my feelings in a safe and supportive environment, and, most importantly, prioritize my own wellness while continuing to be an empathic and passionate caregiver to my mom. Although she eventually no longer knew who I was, my spirit learned how to be more peaceful on the journey alongside her.

I was five months pregnant with my daughter in August of 1999. One Sunday morning, I received sombre news that my dad had gone into cardiac arrest while helping out in a neighbor's garden. Despite the courageous efforts of his neighbor in administering CPR, my dad likely passed away before the paramedics even arrived. This sudden loss left me reeling and stumbling about in a desperate dance for normalcy.

Two months later, I experienced life-threatening complications, which led to an emergency c-section followed by an exploratory surgery to determine why my body unexpectedly began shutting down and rejecting the pregnancy. With no conclusive answers, my focus quickly shifted to caring for my daughter during her five-week recovery period in the NICU while I also continued to heal. Incidentally, that little one has grown into a phenomenal young lady who is courageously navigating her own incredible life story.

The progressive loss of a loved one, through the devastatingly slow degeneration of their personality and essence, is a very different experience from that of a sudden death. The larcenous spectre of dementia lurks in the halls of the mind, indiscriminately tossing out memories and replacing them with random snippets of a wonderful life mingled with whimsical recollections. It is a vicious beast, relentlessly intent on erasing bits and pieces of that beautiful soul until, eventually, nothing familiar remains.

In reflecting on my experience, I don't know whether greater comfort is found in the granting of a longer, more rehearsed, farewell or in the grace of an unexpected departure. Neither is an easy road to travel for those left to mourn. What I do know, is that each offers valuable lessons in keeping our hearts open and loving one another and especially ourselves, while remaining focused on finding our inner peace and reconnecting with our joy in the midst of our sorrow.

As the shock of my dad's passing began to ease, my mom soon settled into a new routine. She was determined to continue "doing what she could until she could do no longer"—a personal creed of hers, no doubt the result of her stoic British upbringing. She had been shaped by a series of life-altering events that had impacted her early childhood: the loss of her father when she was a toddler, the witnessing of a step-father's abusive behavior, and the physical separation from her mother and baby sister when she went to live with a beloved uncle and aunt. All of these experiences occurred before her fourteenth birthday, while under the austere and traumatic conditions of World War II. After graduating with honours from finishing school, her strong work ethic enabled her to forge a reputation as an outstanding administrator. She was a truly remarkable woman who, after meeting and marrying the love of her life, immigrated to Canada, inspired to raise a family under much different circumstances than either had experienced as children.

Upon establishing themselves in Calgary, my parents soon settled into a new way of life and started a family. As my brother and I grew to be more independent, travelling became one of their favourite pursuits; one that eventually led them to the enchanting islands of Hawai'i. The warm weather, exotic flowers, and sandy shores lured them back to Maui for many years; it became their tropical sanctuary at the tail-end of Calgary's chilly winters. Maui was a place of such deep connection for them that, when the grandkids were born, my mom became known as *Tūtū*, a Hawaiian term for grandparent. In April, following my dad's passing, we sought refuge on the island to continue healing as a family. I also hoped to create new memories that would help my mom to once again find joy in the places my parents had loved so much.

As the years progressed, my mom and I enjoyed several opportunities to escape the bitter cold together. It was on one of these trips back to Maui in early 2006 that I really began noticing changes in her behaviour. Knowing the pantry and fridge of our rental apartment would be empty, it was routine for us to grocery shop upon arrival. However, this time was different: she had, what I perceived to

95

be, an irrational panic attack. While browsing the shelves, she seemed to be taking longer than usual and I could feel my frustration rising at her inability to make a "simple" decision. Casually mentioning that I was going to get a loaf of bread, I suggested that she take her time and that we meet up in the next aisle. A few moments later, I heard her loudly calling my name as she frantically paced the end of the aisles trying to track me down. Shortly thereafter, we argued in front of the frozen entrees. She was adamant that we had a freezer full of stuff "back home," which needed to be finished before we bought anything new. Although these incidents did not prevent us from thoroughly enjoying the rest of our time together, I struggled to convince myself that this strange episode had been brought on by jetlag and I was unable to shake a sense of foreboding.

The changes were very gradual at first, but as time passed, more and more "little things" began to happen, raising concern about her mental health. In late October 2007, my mother-in-law invited me to attend an open house about dementia put on by the Calgary Alzheimer's Society of Calgary. She knew that I was troubled by my mom's increasingly strange behaviour and that I was afraid to ask the hard questions. I wasn't ready to admit what we could possibly be facing, but after all of the routine medical testing had come back normal, there seemed to be no other explanation.

We listened to the presenter talk about the different types of dementia, early indications, potential stages, and available medications. During a brief intermission, when I quietly commented that I recognized my mom in some of what the speaker had described, I felt a gently placed hand on my forearm and heard the softly spoken words "This was why I wanted to bring you." That was the unequivocal moment when I made the gut-wrenching connection between my mom's increasingly odd behavior and dementia; it was no longer a "remote possibility" but a "most likely scenario." I spent the remainder of the program vainly trying to suppress my emotions as I tearfully questioned the speaker about getting a definitive diagnosis and the availability of resources. I walked out of that session in a daze, overwhelmed by such an emotional revelation, but armed with a stubborn resolve to learn more about this cruel disease and the havoc it was about to wreak upon our family.

Shortly thereafter, my brother and I discussed our concerns with my mom's physician, and we began putting together a more comprehensive care plan. My mom went through numerous medical assessments, which led to several pharmaceutical and nutritional adjustments. In addition, my brother and I began providing increased support for day-to-day activities while closely monitoring and documenting changes in her cognitive abilities. Our collective efforts enabled her to continue living safely in the familiarity of her own home until a year later when she received a more conclusive diagnosis of irreversible dementia, most likely Alzheimer's disease. One of many types of dementia, Alzheimer's is a degenerative neurological disease that progressively attacks healthy brain tissue, impacting a person's cognitive and functional abilities, affecting moods and emotions, changing personality characteristics, and impairing physical mobility. During the final, end-of-life stage of the disease, bodily functions begin to shut down, ultimately resulting in death.

At this point, I recognized that I needed to gain greater perspective. My husband and I started by attending a series of seminars at the Society. We spent many hours reading, sharing, and absorbing the inescapable reality of what was to come. Along with other families, we spent several months learning about what resources and reliable sources of information were available. In addition, we were encouraged to seek emotional support for ourselves as part of our caregiving responsibilities. Our seminar group soon came to realize that, although some of our experiences were comparable, the disease impacted each of our loved ones in very unique ways. Despite the differences, however, what we all shared, was a common desire to learn how to navigate the rocky rapids ahead with our loved ones, as safely and compassionately as possible.

Looking back, it's hard to believe everything that happened over a few short years. With the continued love and support of close friends and extended family, together we weathered many emotionally challenging phases of this disease as it progressed. The first major adjustment came with packing up my mom's cherished home and moving her into an assisted-living apartment. That move was followed by several more relocations, from assisted-living to a memory care unit, then on to an out-of-town behavioral assessment facility, and finally, to a wonderful specialty-care residence. I learned many lessons in the course of this transformational experience. I learned that my relationship with my mom had to change; I was now the caregiver in our parent-child relationship. I learned to become a respectful and assertive advocate for her when communicating with health care professionals and dealing with administrative procedures. I learned to practice living in the moment, especially when our respective realities didn't coincide. Most significantly, I learned the art of how not to take things personally.

For the longest time, I have kept a journal, purposefully recording the joyful, the sorrowful, and the mundane moments of raising a family, especially the various traveling escapades upon which we embarked either as a family or just with my mom, one-on-one. As her illness progressed, I desperately needed an outlet for sharing the ugliness that often welled up inside me and my journal gave me a safe place to express my feelings. I was terrified of shedding light upon the truly awful episodes. Not only did I fear reproach, I feared embarrassment, and the guilt I felt over struggling to cope was difficult to accept. Only through a great deal of self-compassion, therapy, and personal coaching did I begin feeling brave enough to open up about these experiences.

In early 2015, I started revisiting some of those harsher episodes to reflect upon the power I had given them. It was time for me to learn the art of personal forgiveness so that I could truly begin to heal my heart. What follows is an excerpt from my journal and some other memories that served as points of reflection on my journey to wellness.

May 17, 2010

"... before picking up my mom for dinner. Rich made a fantastic BBQ steak feast, and everyone ate to their heart's content. It was going on 10:00 by the time I dropped her back off at the apartment. I really made an effort to let her tell her stories more than once and tried not to correct her. Not much point is there and if it makes her happy to reminisce even if not quite accurate— who really cares? I know she was pretty tired by the time we were done so I'm sure she settled in quickly and went off to sleep. It's hard sometimes to hear her go on about how she is locked in and never gets chance to go outside for walks very much but I wonder how much of that is really true now that nicer weather is here? I think sometimes she doesn't remember how often Ray and Pam (my brother and sister-in-law) take her out and about or the staff during the day or even me on the odd occasion. I have to admit that some days are definitely easier than others—I just have to have the right mind-set to manage so I am able to side-step the rabbit hole. I often wonder how many other people such as myself go through these types of emotions—I know I'm not the only one but it would be interesting to know how they choose to cope. Are they also journal writers, wine drinkers and food stuffers?"

A Fit of Rage

I remember once sitting in my vehicle at the doctor's office. I had just come from a frustrating appointment to renew my mom's memory medication and the amount of red tape I had been forced to endure was too much for me. I had reached my saturation point. After politely leaving the office, I barely made it inside my van before the emotional storm broke. I slammed the door and began pounding my fists on the steering wheel while screaming as loudly as I could, *"FOR F*** SAKE! Just give me a break here! Is. It. Too. Much. To. Ask?"* There I sat, crumpled over the steering wheel, shoulders heaving, unable to stem the flow of tears or catch my breath as the rage consumed me. Eventually my fury dissipated, and I regained enough composure to continue on with my day.

A Gift from the Universe

Shortly after relocating my mom to the assisted-living facility, friends and family began packing up the remainder of her personal effects in preparation for the sale of her home. One day, while doing a final check to ensure nothing was missed, the Universe revealed a gift. High up on my parents' bedroom closet shelf, I found the remnants of a Halloween costume: a hand-made magic wand. The star was fashioned from a piece of cardboard, wrapped in tinfoil, and fastened to the end of a wooden dowel. My dad had been a creative character with a talent for making imagination-fueling props for us kids. I had completely forgotten about this piece of wizardry, but the moment my fingers wrapped around it, a flood of wonderful memories came rushing in. At first, I just stood there, feeling overcome by the reality of all that had transpired then slowly I began waving it about as I traipsed through the rest of the house, loudly humming the song *Put it Together* from Cinderella. It was my way of banishing the sad memories and imparting blessings of joyful energy to the new owners. Thank goodness there was no one else around to witness my little fit of lunacy: it can be tough enough keeping up appearances without anyone learning about my fairy godmother tendencies!

A Place of Quiet Resignation

Over the years, my mom's mobility slowly declined but, as I discovered, it is extremely difficult to teach someone with impaired cognition how to use a walker because they are unable to retain new information. Unfortunately, her physical instability resulted in her breaking first her left, then her right hip, on separate occasions, which led to two different surgeries and two very different recoveries. The first time, when she was lying on the gurney in the emergency ward, writhing in pain, I felt so helpless while the team waited on the surgeon's assessment to medicate her. It's hard for me to admit that I silently pleaded with the Universe to help her, even if it meant I had to lose her right then and there. Once sedated, she quickly drifted off, the wild-eyed panic replaced by a catatonic state, a haunting vision that lingers in my mind to this day. The surgeon warned us that given her age and health concerns, there was a significant possibility that she would not survive the surgery. At that moment I silently encouraged the Universe to guide her gently whichever way it chose.

Amazingly, her recovery was quite swift. Thanks to physiotherapy and the help of her incredible care team, she was up and about in record time, racking up the miles during her daily energetic hallway walk-a-thons. The second break came about a year later. Though seemingly less painful and dramatic, the inevitable surgery that followed wound up limiting her mobility even further until she was completely wheelchair bound.

One of the most important lessons I learned as a caregiver, is that the role is challenging and can often lead to a dark place. If you don't remember to take care of yourself, it can be difficult to develop healthy coping mechanisms to get you through the tough times. Caregiver burnout is not pretty; it is especially common among people who already tend to put others before themselves and have difficulty asking for help. For too long, I was afraid of opening my own "Pandora's box" because the idea of losing "control" of my emotions and appearing weak, vulnerable, or selfish, terrified me. Being unable to provide support to my loved ones in their times of need, equaled failure in my eyes—even if it came at the expense of my own wellbeing.

If you are a caregiver for someone with dementia, it is important to know that you are not alone. Organizations like the Calgary Alzheimer's Society and the Family Caregiver Centre are great resources to contact for support along with traditional forms of talk therapy such as grief therapy, psychotherapy, and group therapy among others. Experimenting with different types of physical activity can also help release some of that emotional s**t. Try yoga, drumming, dancing, weight-training, or even learning how to break boards with your bare hands in tae kwon-do as I did. The key is to find healthy ways of coping to deal with the additional stress brought on by your situation.

Other, less traditional, methods of self-care include: maintaining a dark sense of humor in the midst of your despair, finding an amazing group of humans with whom to connect and share your stories, or simply manifesting a personal prayer and request for help from the Universe using the power of your words. When it comes to prayer, it really doesn't matter whether you vocalize it by screaming from the top of your lungs in a fit of rage or by whispering it under your breath, from a place of quiet resignation—just ask.

My purpose in sharing our story is to provide encouragement to those of you faced with a similar heart-task. Asking for help can feel intimidating but doing so is *not* a sign of weakness or selfishness. Remembering to care for yourself is the most loving thing you can do to re-establish your inner balance and to continue providing care for those you love.

E Mālama Pono

(Take good care and be well)

Lessons Learned:

1. Develop Thick Skin

Many times, I bore the brunt of my mom's frustration with her memory loss, and was often accused of being disrespectful, cruel, even spiteful. By recognizing that her behavior was the result of the changes going on in her brain, and not a reflection of how she truly felt, I was able to let the hurtful comments come and go without taking them personally.

2. Reminisce Creatively

Releasing the desire to bring my mom back into *my* present reality became an opportunity for us to reminisce creatively about our adventures through shared storytelling. Over time, learning how to meet her where (and as who) she was at any given moment, became more important than getting hung up on her internal visions and fantastical retelling of life-events.

3. Not Forever, Just for Now

This has become my personal mantra for persevering through life's challenges. I recognize and accept whatever difficulty I am currently facing and find solace in the knowledge that the experience won't last forever. I remind myself that change is inevitable.

4. Shift Focus

Being a caregiver introduced whole new levels of stress and anxiety to my life, so I began to explore various forms of supportive therapy. By engaging in activities that required a shift in focus, I was able to release some of my pent-up energy—I often felt physically tired but mentally energized after spending time moving my body and getting out of my head.

5. Give Grace/Hold Space

During difficult times, I often found it easier to give grace and hold space for others than for myself. Learning to cultivate that compassion and empathy for myself, has helped me to nurture that little kid in me who was deeply grieving the loss of her parents.

Mindset Tips:

When you are struggling, try one (or all) of the following suggestions to clear the stagnant energy that keeps you mired in repetitive patterns of negative thoughts and feelings:

1. Write It Out - put pen to paper and journal whatever comes to mind.
2. Seek It Out – explore healthy ways of coping with challenges.
3. Talk It Out - find a safe environment to share your experiences.
4. Work It Out – get out of your head and into your body by moving.
5. Laugh It Out – discover the humour hidden in the moment.

A-ha Moments and Self-Reflections

Note your Thoughts

_____

_____

_____

_____

_____

_____

_____

_____

_____

_____

_____

_____

_____

_____

_____

_____

_____

_____

_____

_____

_____

Allison Tuffs

Allison is a certified high-performance coach, nutritionist, author, and speaker. She is on a mission to help women redefine themselves and their lives after loss.

Loss changes you at your core, it affects your whole life, and not just for a moment but for a lifetime. It changes how you look at the world and how you see yourself in it.

Following the loss of her daughter, Allison experienced years of pain, exhaustion, and life dissatisfaction. Her journey has been both challenging and fulfilling. She now lives pain free and helps other women walk the journey of discovering who they are after loss, what they're going to do now, and how to live a fully energized and fulfilled life, while fully acknowledging their loss.

Connect with Allison:
Allison@AllisonTuffs.com
www.Allisontuffs.com
https://www.facebook.com/UpYourEnergy/

Chapter 8:

Let Your Breath Be Your Guide

By Allison Tuffs

What's Balance Got to Do with life? In pondering the meaning of balance, the obvious comes to mind: the dance of yin and yang, sweet and salty, silky smooth and crunchy. Between two extremes, the sweet spot lives in the balance.

I'm a performance and potential coach, with a nutrition background, so I find balance in how a delicious meal comes together, for example: the sensations of how foods dance on the palate. For me, the complexity of flavors and textures is the difference between an ok meal and a delicious one. One need only think of one's favorite meal and the joy each bite brings. Given the opportunity, most people would choose the best tasting foods on offer, with a secondary consideration to how healthy it is.

Most of us can easily relate to that form of balance, and maybe at its core, that is the easiest way to explain this construct called balance.

Yet when we dig deeper, balance is more complex. It is about finding peace in the midst of the storms we face in life. Balance is about remaining true to the person we see in the mirror. It is about being internally centered and remaining true to who we are at our core.

Why do we need balance? Because as the external world swirls around us, how we respond to the obstacles we find in our path, that threaten to swallow us and throw our inner compass off, is key to our happiness. If our response to life is a knee-jerk reaction, we lose something very precious: our sense of balance, calm, and joy.

Have you ever felt overwhelmed, frazzled, completely rattled, or for lack of a better word, triggered? I have. And not for a day or a week, but for years. The impact on my life was significant: gradually my temper became short, my stomach began to hurt all the time, and my memory declined. Not to mention the loss of sleep and passion as a result of the stress. In my experience, these are all common symptoms of a loss of balance.

For me, the questions became: how do I return to balance? How do I reconnect to the moment, to my heart, my body and my life, when I am constantly feeling uncentered?

I tried everything, from exercise, yoga, and self-medicating to meditation. They were all great practices, with the exception of self-medicating (also known as self-sabotage), but none of them were quite the solution I was looking for. After much experimentation, I discovered that the most effective technique for me involves the use of breath, which is quick, free, and available twenty-four-seven. Simply focusing on what is happening with my breathing helps me to drop back into my body, make adjustments and re-establish balance.

Breath is always with us, and when we choose to tune in, it is all telling. For example, fast and shallow breathing tells us that we are stressed out, or possibly scared and out of balance.

Even when our world is calm and life is ticking along: we have a good career, our children are happy, our relationships are sound, and our desires are met, we can fall out of balance. For me, even here in my utopia, all it takes is for me to drop one of the balls I am juggling, and, *bam,* I'm scrambling; *boom,* I'm out of balance.

People offer up the concept of self-care as a prescription for balance. I have to tell you, I love self-care, I do, but *seriously,* when we're out of balance for whatever reason, do we really have time to curl up with a good book? Find quiet time in the bathtub? Do you?

What I *do* have time for, is turning my awareness inward to my breath. I have time to consciously commit to a long slow inhale, followed by a longer, slower exhale. I do this several times and I notice a shift, a releasing of my shoulders, a quieting of my spinning mind, a centering and redirecting of my thoughts. These are all good outcomes that I can achieve at anytime: when I'm driving, when I'm in a meeting, when the kids are irritating the heck out of me. You get the idea.

I first discovered this breathing technique when my world crashed ten years ago. My daughter died. That moment took my breath away for months. Make that years. Healing and balance returned as I committed to tuning into my breath, to redefining who I am versus the vision I had of who I would be as a mother of four.

Tragedy is awful. Its gift comes as the fog of pain and sorrow lifts. Sometimes just enough to take a breath and make a choice about how you want to live. For me, it was a pull: as if an external force was drawing me out of the pain and swirling thoughts, drawing me toward a light. At first, it was pure necessity that caused me to seek healing, but over time, the desire to find lasting inner peace, to rediscover my inner passion, and to have the energy to experience life's full spectrum of joys and challenges became the impetus for my continued search for healing and balance.

Prioritizing balance is a daily decision that causes me to be fully connected to scheduled tasks and life. Recently my Aunt passed, which brought up strong emotions, some of which, to my surprise, were also tied to the loss of my daughter. Because breath awareness has become a habit, I was able to tune into the moments where I held, shortened, or quickened my breath. Once aware, I could stop, take a few deep slow breaths to regain balance and do some self-evaluation, ask questions, and address the unresolved emotions.

Is breath awareness easy? Not always because it requires us to stay consciously connected to ourselves and life. If you've ever driven home and forgotten the drive, you might be living on autopilot and not be consciously connected. Have you done this? I have. And in my experience, rarely does anything good come from being in my head, disconnected, and often ruminating.

For me, a better way of responding to life's crests and troughs is to shift my perspective. This is possible when I connect to my breath and consciously connect with what is happening. I believe we are more resilient when we connect to our breath, and when we are, it's easier to find this delicate thing called "balance." Life is better when we feel balanced.

People say, "fake it until you make it." I tried and found that I could fake it to the external world, but I couldn't fake it on the inside, the only place that matters. You see, when you look in the mirror, the person that stares back at you knows unequivocally if you're in balance or not.

Life will continue to present obstacles and throw challenges my way. Some will be harder than others, but if I allow breath to be my lighthouse, I will be able to find balance even when the going gets tough. I don't have it all figured out, but I do know this.

I'm learning to be gentle with myself. On those days when life isn't good, you know those days we all have, I focus on finding a moment to just breathe, to slow my world down, and focus on the inhale and exhale. Sometimes I walk and simply saying to myself, *inhale, exhale*; this alone can be enough to reconnect with myself and allow a shift in perspective of how I see the craziness of life.

Connecting to breath has allowed me to understand that I have thoughts, but that I am not my thoughts. That I have pain, but I am not my pain. Breath restores, calms, and creates space for my brain to quiet. That is balance.

With balance, my step becomes lighter, and the world starts to shift and look oh so slightly different. Others may not notice, but for me, internally it feels different and that's all that matters.

Life is a teeter-totter between the good and bad, the yin and yang, the sweet and salty. One without the other would rob us of the incredible experience life has to offer. I don't want to pass through life, I want to fully engage in it. I want to feel passion and experience its full breadth and depth. Do you?

I believe that balance matters, and I seek it out each day. You matter, and my hope is that by sharing my story I can inspire you to find hope and balance in your own breath and in your own life.

Lessons Learned:

1. Follow peace, aka balance
   - Command your mind by controlling your breath
   - Keep your promises to yourself as well as others. I'm always working on this.
   - Seek a trusted voice to share your thoughts and feeling with.
   - Take action: take a breath, calm your mind, and then step into your next move.
2. Find your passion and love your life. Be realistic. You're never going to love 100% of everything you do, but you can find the joy, passion, and fulfillment in what you do.
3. Believe in yourself and what you're doing, then stay out of your head (unless engaged in strategic thinking). When "what if" thinking kicks in, take a breath, shift your perspective, and check back to see if you're still on point. Are you still loving it? Do you still believe in its value?

Mindset Tips:

1. Stay positive by checking in regularly with your breath. Is it sticking anywhere in your body? Are you holding it in? Is it deep or shallow? Simply inhale to a count and exhale to a slightly longer count to drop back into your body and get centered.
2. Live this moment, life is in the now. Yesterday has passed, and you can't control tomorrow. Be present in your actions by staying out of your head. Pinch yourself if you must, but be present.
3. Slow down. This is a gift you can give yourself. Stop to smell the roses, walk in nature, and disconnect from the digital world.

A-ha Moments and Self-Reflections

Note your Thoughts

_____

_____

_____

_____

_____

_____

_____

_____

_____

_____

_____

_____

_____

_____

_____

_____

_____

_____

_____

_____

_____

Heather Andrews, Compiler

Heather Andrews is a publisher, international best-selling author, and speaker. After writing her first book, Heather saw firsthand how stories foster hope and change lives. It became apparent to her that the process of writing and sharing compelling stories is a transformational one, for both the audience and the author. The profound healing that Heather both felt and observed after publishing her first book was a monumental sign. Through her own re-discovery of self-esteem and her journey to the realization of a deeper personal identity based on values rather than just a prestigious job title, Heather knew she needed to help others like her get their powerful stories in front of those who needed them most.

Heather is a sought-after conference speaker who inspires audiences in her own direct and dynamic manner by sharing her challenges and survival strategies that continue to help her optimize adversity. A voice for self-discovery and fearless revitalization, Heather always makes a positive difference.

Connect with Heather:
www.getyouvisible.com
www.facebook.com/getyouvisible
www.linkedin.com/andrewsheather

Chapter 9:

Balance: A Creation of Your Own Story

"You are the creator of your own story."

–Heather Andrews

Do you remember playing on a teeter-totter, a long narrow board that pivots up and down in the middle? Imagine me as an eight-year-old, standing in the middle of the teeter-totter trying to balance it so it lays straight. With my tiny feet, I put a little more weight on one side and then slowly shift them to the other side to hold the board straight. It takes a lot of effort to hold it straight and keep it balanced. One of my friends runs over, laughs, and pushes up one end...leaving me to balance it all over again. Little did I know it back then, but as an eight-year-old, I was developing the act of resiliency for life!

Balance in any area of life is much like that teeter-totter—it has ups and downs, with moments of keeping life seemingly equal on both sides. Then something, or someone, comes along to throw you off balance. Does that sound familiar?

Balance is never status quo. Maybe on the 1950s TV show, "Father Knows Best" problems were solved in thirty minutes or less so that daily life had a happy ending. The reality was there were turbulent times, even for the "Brady Bunch" family—it just wasn't always talked about. After all these years, one would think that we would have all the answers to the mystical search to create balance in our lives like the "normal" people on TV. But much like keeping the teeter-totter straight, life balance continues to change daily, weekly, monthly, and yearly—and is rarely achieved in only thirty minutes.

My question as I compiled this book was: "Is balance achievable in today's world?" I believe it is. The meaning of the word and how it is viewed is what needs to change. When I look back on my journey, there are so many things I wish I'd known. I've learned many lessons, often the hard way, about the meaning of balance and how to achieve it.

Lesson #1: Give up the comparison theory—do it your way

Above all else, forgiveness and kindness toward the self needs to be prioritized. Meanwhile, the opinions of others can be swiftly booted curbside. Who is the *judgment committee* in your life? I can honestly say the people who judge me for anything I haven't given them permission to, no longer have space in my life. End of story. If they are not part of my committee, I put them into a box of boundaries. I limit how much access they have to me and how often I am around them.

I learned that about fifteen years ago in my mid-thirties when my children's father deployed to Afghanistan during our marriage. I was working full time with a thriving business. Our children were eight, five, and three during the first deployment. The original news came as a huge shock, and we only had six weeks to plan for an eighteen-month deployment. Naturally, as a *modern day* woman, I figured I could do it all.

That worked for all of two months! I gained twenty pounds from drive thru food and soda, suffered high levels of stress, drove my kids to activities seven days a week, and was working and running my company. Exhaustion set in. I feared being judged as weak or that I couldn't do it all if I asked for help. It took one trip to the emergency room from chest pain at thirty-five years old to make me realize "I'm the only parent my kids have while their dad is serving for eighteen months, so I best get my sh*t together."

In the days following, I emptied our calendar and cancelled all activities. I restructured my company so I could the do private group events at my house to limit my time away and leverage it better.

I sat down with the kids to find out what activities they enjoyed, and they had to select two. I was able to put them into group activities like swimming at the same time. While they had fun, I hit the gym. Time opened up on the weekend to meal prep and do a fun family activity. We went to bed at the same time each night so we all got rest. Shocking as it was—my kids were less cranky, and so was I. There was downtime and time for fun.

Lesson #2: Make yourself your accountability partner

During this time of life balance, no one cared that I overhauled my calendar. Everyone else was in their own swirl and trying to exist in their own chaos.

As the months passed, there were still moments of chaos, but I had a handle on it and awareness when life started to spiral downward. I knew it was time to take a step back to see what was working and what needed changing. I communicated with my kids even though they were super young. We often don't think our kids know what they want, but if you listen and ask, they will tell you. Sometimes kids know best, and it's important to listen to them in order to learn. Even my five-year-old daughter said, "Why don't you ask for help?" Like, *Duh*—so I asked...and my life changed.

The deployment came to an end—their dad came home to a new family foundation and a home running like a well-oiled unit. Setting boundaries, learning to communicate in a different way, and being open to asking for help—and better yet, receiving it—were the life savers for what had been uncontrolled chaos. The lessons learned set a precedent for my kids, and we all gained a better understanding of boundaries and stress management.

As mothers, we lead by example. If we are a stressed-out mess, that is okay for the moment. But if it continues, what are we teaching our children? The day I collapsed in the ER was a wake-up call for me... and it scared them. My question is: "Why do we need to have a complete wake-up call or hit rock bottom, so to speak, before we change anything?"

Lesson #3: Obstacles teach us many things to prepare us for more

Two years later, the news of the second deployment came. This time, we had the tools and strategies in place, and it was our new autopilot, so to speak.

The secret to balance is to know that you and your family unit, whatever that looks like, have your own definition of balance that *works for you*. There is no comparison with others for any of it. As the world of social media explodes, we see each person's highlight reel of their life that makes them look like they are doing so well. However, I can tell you from experience that most are drowning, and those who aren't have figured out what support they need to keep balance in the ever-changing landscape of their life.

Curve balls are thrown throughout your entire life, and even if no curve balls are coming at you right now, your kids and your life are always changing with age, new circumstances, pivots in business or your workplace, loss of family and friends, financial gains and setbacks, health issues and the list goes on. We can get comfortable and stuck in our balance routine, thinking that what we have always done will work for every curve ball.

The key is learning that what we have always done does not always work. We may need to change direction or apply a different approach or way of doing things. In basketball, when the ball gets passed to you, you need to pivot and look around to see if you should shoot a basket or who you can pass the ball on to at that moment to help you. You work as a team to move the ball forward. Asking for help is an act of empowerment. We weren't meant to walk some of these moments alone.

As the years passed, little did I know that the foundation set in the first year of the deployment would determine how I dealt with boundaries, communication and stress in the years to follow as I raised my kids, changed my careers, and did not listen to other people's judgments. It made me stronger, less stressed, and more productive—a model for my kids.

Lesson #4: You are as important as everyone else in your life

I made myself a priority after realizing that I was just as important as everyone else in my life. I was their mom, not their doormat, and I did not have anything to prove by being a martyr and killing myself. My internal dialogue had to change because there were days when I thought, "I'm not a good enough mom, and I'm failing at my job." The constant criticism from negative self-talk led to a lack of internal peace and contributed to my aforementioned (and legendary) trip to the ER at thirty-five.

After the second deployment, life progressed for me with career advancement to a healthcare manager. I had more responsibility to communicate and carried both a work cell phone and a personal one. If that didn't knock me off balance, I don't know what else would. My life was on call 24/7! Work would start at 6:00 a.m. with employee sick calls and sometimes end at midnight with project updates. There was no life balance, and work became priority over family.

Yes, I know...I allowed this to happen, but I wanted to be available and present like my single male counterparts. Thank goodness my kids were thirteen, ten, and eight by that time. They could stay with their dad or alone—whatever was required—because work came first, as the job paid well. It was not long until the *wellness strategies* I figured out and had implemented during the deployments were flushed down the toilet.

The need to be available took over my life. In retrospect, I allowed it because I didn't speak up from fear of being replaced. Maybe the outcome could have been different, but the fear I could lose my job if I didn't always show up was overwhelming, and I didn't want to let my employer, family, or anyone down. My boss was a good man, and he would have listened if I had shared my concerns and had some solutions.

But this was my issue—my job meant more to me than my family or my wellness, and it made me wonder how many other people sacrifice for the sake of a job? I knew the answer, and needless to say it was many. I told myself *I had balance,* but I was in denial. My dream job became my identity. I was a mid-ranking manager, truly loved my team, and told myself "To have your dream job, you must sacrifice something."

That was my story, and it gradually became my nightmare. My health took a steady decline, and I was diagnosed with high blood pressure and a heart issue. I stopped exercising, was drinking wine daily, and ate more processed food than ever before. One would have thought I learned my lesson years before from my trip to ER, but that was not the case.

I was put on medication and suffered through a year's worth of testing. Once again, I began meal prepping and started an exercise program called Beachbody®. I lost weight and loved the company so much I joined their movement as a health coach to help others begin their health journeys. I was learning that *health is wealth*—the condition of our health impacts how we show up in every other aspect of our lives. I began to understand that as we get busy or face adversity, the first important priority to go out the window is exercise—but truly, it is the last activity we should eliminate.

My job was killing my body and soul...I needed something for my creative side. I loved this wellness journey so much I enrolled in a course to become a certified coach. Little did I know this would be the beginning of a major life shift and the birth of my company, Follow It Thru.

For years I took numerous valuable courses for management and leadership including content on conflict, communication, team building, difficult conversations, key performance indicators, project management and change management. But nothing prepared me for the health life-coaching course, as this one required us to deal with our *own* mindset, beliefs and habits before we could go on to coach others.

As I began this course, my life was so off balance—I was in survivor mode, and close to the point of burn out. My dream job had become very stressful due to internal changes, and I really did not know what my future held. Intuition told me daily that it could be my last day of work. I prayed it wouldn't be, but was absolutely fed up with the churning feeling in my stomach knowing each day could be my last as I walked into work. That dreaded day finally came to fruition...

I was in a staff meeting when my co-worker knocked on the door. "Human Resources wants to see you." My heart sank—this was the beginning of the end. I finished my meeting and slowly headed over to the department. All the doors were closed as I silently walked down the long hallway to the boardroom. I took a deep breath and slowly opened the heavy door. The HR manager was sitting there behind her large desk, staring coldly at me with the look of death on her face. We had worked together for thirteen years, but that didn't seem to matter at the moment. As I nervously sat down, she slid the brown envelope on the desk across to me. "Thank you for your service. We are restructuring. Goodbye and good luck." Boom! Thirteen years of sacrifice...GONE.

I somehow felt strong as I drove home. But I was in a daze. As I pulled up in the driveway, the reality hit me like a wrecking ball. "I'm unemployed for the first time...ever!" In that moment, I went from the top of my dream job world to the bottom of the unemployment lake. The second bomb went off. "How am I going to tell my family and kids that I don't have a job anymore?" Talk about feeling like a failure. My mind was racing. "How will I convince them not to worry? I'm the family breadwinner, and they know it."

This curve ball was an opportunity for new balance and a new perspective on life. There were rushes of pity and anger but then remarkable strength because "I am NOT a failure nor am I going to let this sink me!"

The survivor and fighter in me applied for every job. I reached out to every connection that I knew to gain contracts and casual work. The key insight I gained was that I knew I had been given the gift of a second chance, despite the situation and feelings of loss. The main action that saved me was the fact I was still in my coaching course and applying so much of what I learned to my own life. I realized that what I was feeling was super natural, and I gave myself permission to feel the emotions for the first time ever. I was meant to do something different...and it was *time to do it!*

Nineteen days later, I was back at work with two contracts. It was then that I decided to create my own coaching company. A balancing act for this new beginning was created and performed for the next four years.

I was so darn excited to create my business from scratch, but little did I know what lay ahead. As my dream unfolded, I made countless mistakes, had many priceless opportunities open up, experienced pitfalls and obstacles and embraced moments of lessons learned. There were people I met who taught me valuable lessons and others who literally sucked the life out of me. I saw the rolls of the eyes from those who thought I was crazy or could not understand my dream or my big vision. This new business and big dream required my time, but also a significant investment of money.

Lessons 5 to 11 were learned from 2016 to 2019.

I completed my coaching certificate in 2016, and I thought it would be so easy to gain clients. Despite what the Facebook ads advertised, and I believed, the clients did not magically come, so I continued to work my J-O-B. I hired a couple of business coaches to help me get my business off the ground. One told me to monitor my money, budget, and manage growth. The other coach was able to help create a brand and online platform. Both were very different focuses and both correct and valuable in their own way. I applied the principles that each of them taught me to leverage my business. I invested in myself and business...this has paid off multiple times over the years.

In my first year, I grew my brand, Follow It Thru coaching. It helped women navigate through the unbalanced overwhelm of their life and career. They learned to put themselves first to become a better, healthier version of themselves and successfully manage stress. As I grew this brand, I continued to invest and create my company.

Between work, my company, and my three kids, there was no time for much else. Even though I taught health, self-care, and stress management, I did not listen to my own teachings. In the entrepreneurial world we speak of *alignment*. If you aren't living truth to what you are teaching, it affects your energy, how people are drawn to you, and whether they hire you or not. Your potential clients can *sense* these energies, and frequently act on them. Being transparent is about the vulnerability you share, how you relate to your potential clients, how you make them feel and whether they feel like they can trust you.

People need to trust you; but if you can't trust yourself to carry out your own teachings, how can they? The shift that occurred here was when I worked for someone else, I knew my role, my job description, and the expectations. In the world of entrepreneurism, people buy YOU—the relationship they have with you—not your product, per se. The kicker was, in my own company, I did not know my role or job description, nor did I have any expectations in that space.

This lack of understanding became very evident when I spoke in Miami about my story and coaching program. I stood on the stage at a high-end hotel with 100 female entrepreneurs looking to me to provide expert advice on balance. My delivery went well but despite how good my speech was, it was not from my heart—I felt no passion for my coaching company. I had spent $60,000 on coaching, a website, platforms, marketing, etc. and yet thought, "This business is not for me." I got on the plane a day later, feeling depleted.

As I sat on the plane, I thought about life over the last fifteen months from my layoff to this moment where I hit this roadblock in my company. *Holy mother trucker*, this was hard! I had bought into what I believed to be easy from what I read online about the coaching world. "Become a coach and make a six-figure income your first year!" I felt so foolish and wondered what I should do next.

Being an entrepreneur was not what people made it out to be. Owning a company and starting from scratch was difficult! I asked myself: *What do I need to do next?* I spent October and November of 2016 talking to my coaches and trusted friends about why I believed I was a failure, even to the point of considering shutting down my coaching practice because I was struggling to gain clients. However, my gut instinct kept saying, "No, I can't shut it down." I was only just beginning my journey, and I was meant to do more. Deep down I knew that I was not restructured from my job without it having a purpose in my life to move me forward in some way. My mentors guided me through a whirlwind of emotions and self-criticism that were necessary for me to grieve the loss of what I *thought* I wanted. Their guidance and wisdom allowed me to see that I had not failed, and I emerged on the other side of this crisis with new resilience and real clarity around what I *truly* wanted for my company and my life. It was then that I really understood the power of wise counsel, vulnerability and taking meaningful action toward change.

In July 2016, I attended a networking event where I met an amazing lady with a huge vision. As our friendship grew, she introduced me to her friend Mary, a business owner in Texas. Mary asked me, "Would you be interested in sharing your story in a book about building your coaching business?" In that defining moment, I was invited to write in a co-authored book about women building businesses. Although I had built a successful company in my 30s, I was scared to death to let people know the dark side of what I had struggled through. My kids said, "Mom, go do you!" Thankfully, I listened to them...and did the naked me. When *The No BS Guide to Women in Business* hit bestseller on Amazon, it changed my coaching program, the alignment to my company and my new confident belief in myself. I embraced clarity.

This pivotal moment changed Follow It Thru. The publisher reached out and asked, "Would you be interested in a mentorship and publishing a book?" Little did I know that saying, "Yes!" would require another rebalance for my life. A new branch of my company was born. Our first book, *Obstacles Equal Opportunities,* had twenty-two people as co-authors. It launched only two years after my layoff, went bestseller, and Follow It Thru Publishing was born.

When I think of balance during this time, it was my inner belief that changed. My self-worth soared because I was serving others, and our book made a difference to numerous people. Friendships, business partnerships and readers were joined together. It was the foundation for what was to come. All the connections I made, the choices to overcome judgment and fear, and finding clarity by stepping into the alignment of my story to my business was the creation of new balance for my life and company.

The power of my story became my mission, passion, and purpose, which changed the direction of our company. We had to evolve and set a new foundation in place in our transition from coaching to publishing. During 2018 we launched our second compilation, *The Real Journey of the Empowered Momboss*. As working mothers, we learn to embrace imperfection and still make work and family life succeed. I purchased a podcast network and launched my first podcast. The biggest shift came when we launched our first solo book, which gave us another market and client base. Honestly, the moment that I embraced the fact that I could not be perfect in my life and business, people gravitated to my company and services—the vulnerability we shared made us relatable.

In June 2018, I launched the compilation *What's Self Love Got to Do with It?* It was the game changer for our company, for myself as I realized my worth, my value and what I had learned in my business, my coaching, and the inspirational people that were brought together by story.

Remember the eight-year-old on the teeter-totter? Well, I was now thirty-nine and thriving from the life and business lessons I learned, and from what others had taught me. I leaned into the challenge to expand my team. Financially, the company was still not sound because I had not taken time to manage my numbers, so I hired a business manager. We did our first two marketing events and brought on record numbers of people with 95% business growth. Not enough clients or too many can sink your business if you aren't careful. Not forecasting and managing that balance can be detrimental. Numbers are magical in business: they tell you your profit margin, as well as how you should charge for the time you spend both in your company and mentoring your clients. This lesson in balancing a budget was crucial.

Like many entrepreneurs, I have faced difficult situations financially, emotionally, mentally, and physically while building my company, working, and managing family. The subsequent decisions were based on my life, company, and family. That is why I say balance is an *individual concept*, and to compare yourself to others is a waste of time and limits your opportunities for success. Don't try to climb on and balance my teeter-totter...find your own.

The year 2019 was one of *trust*, *surrender*, and *elevation*.

Trust - I have learned to trust myself, my intuition, and I know what I can create and am capable of. I had to practice my faith and trust in knowing God would provide an answer.

Surrender - I surrender to the wisdom of others and follow the signs of the path that has been put before me. There are signs of confirmation about our path, our life, when we are open enough and aware to pay attention to them. Everything always pointed back to my company.

Elevation - I have elevated my belief in God and Universe. It has served me well as I have more peace and awareness of my vision and message for this world. I am the messenger to share that we are to embrace our own story. Each of us has travelled our unique journey that will help inspire others to know how they can bring hope to others.

These changes have led me to meet so many different people and opportunities. Some of those results are:

- I have travelled extensively speaking in the United States and Canada over twenty times.
- My company was waitlisted for clients as we grew, so we hired a team of editors to support our clients and growth.

- We tripled both the number of authors and volume of books published. We overhauled all of our processes and systems so we can grow effectively to service our clients.
- In the beginning of 2020, we up-leveled our branding, business collaborations, and services to the title Get You Visible.

For every success I have been gutted, and there have been two obstacles to overcome.

As my company and business life thrived, the one obstacle that I did not account for in the balance plan was a major derailment of my personal life. My mom took a serious decline in health. I moved in with her to provide the support she needed. During her illness, I also lost five friends to death. I am strong and resilient, but I had to step into a role for others. I put my own self-care on hold. That lasted for a few months before I hit my wall of disaster.

In that moment, I wisely ASKED for support. I needed to recreate and regenerate my own health so I could balance my life for the growing demands. It was amazing the people that loved, cared for, and supported me when I asked.

As a businesswoman, my life had intense focus, countless responsibilities, financial challenges, and numerous hours away from home. Through all the challenges and learning experiences, I experienced great personal growth. Who I became in the process impacted my marriage. We gradually grew apart, and a new balance plan as a solo parent resulted.

My kids' lives were radically upheaved, but through the love and support of family and friends, we managed this new challenge. Our family looks different now, and everyone is growing and thriving as they seek their own life balance. Change is never easy; it takes courage, faith, and belief to move forward and do the out-of-the-ordinary by others' standard. Most often, there is something better waiting for you. I can attest to that. I have always said, "When one thing is out of sync in your life, chances are other things are too." We can tell ourselves that everything is fine, but sometimes in our gut it just isn't.

I always said the five pillars of life were health, finances, relationships, career, and spirituality. After my job loss, all of them became out of alignment because I changed and my balance definition was gutted. It has taken four years to get the five pillars back in alignment. It is with awareness of consciousness, openness of heart, and learning to trust my gut to know what is right or wrong for my life and those in it that it was able to happen.

This is part of balancing a teeter-totter. Now there is a personal journey for you to discover.

The Final Lesson –You have a choice to connect and create a different culture for your life

It's critical in creating balance to know who you are, what you stand for, how far you can be pushed, and how much you can carry. Healthy balance comes from ongoing awareness of what you tell yourself in the story of your life. You need to ask yourself, "What point, obstacle, or opportunity am I facing now or in the near future?"

As Christmas 2019 drew near, I sat on my couch, a fire crackling, and snow outside my window. I wrote this story to give to you as a present. When you open my gift, it's filled with life experiences and lessons learned that I hope will encourage you to grow and find your unique story. There is this concept called *Balance* and a theory called *You are the Creator of Your Story.* You make a choice to be different and move through your own creation of balance. You own its power for you and your family. You connect to yourself, others, job, or business, and you create a version of something bigger—like your dreams. When you create the story of balance for you and those you love, it is the beginning of the community and culture you desire for your life.

My wish for you, always, is to recognize your power in choice and willingness to change. A well-respected friend shared this quote with me during our conversation about life and choices. I believe it summarizes my chapter on the ups and downs of finding balance in a teeter-totter world.

If you don't like something, change it.

If you cannot change it, accept it.

If you cannot accept it, change it.

Remember to **be you**!! That is the best advice I ever received and was open enough to listen to and implement. ***You are the creator of your own story***. So, go out and create your balance story.

Heather Andrews.

A-ha Moments and Self-Reflections

Note your Thoughts

_____

_____

_____

_____

_____

_____

_____

_____

_____

_____

_____

_____

_____

_____

_____

_____

_____

_____

_____

_____

_____

Conclusion

Your journey with us has come to an end... for now.

We hope that you discovered that we can all find balance in each aspect of our lives, with awareness and perspective.

I hope that what you read between these pages has been insightful and has helped guide you to understand more about the process of achieving balance and its unique importance.

This journey of resetting balance in your life is about loving yourself enough to desire a different outcome, peace and harmony. It is not a one-size-fits-all description. Your balance is unique to you, much like your DNA. It is about being real and asking yourself some very pointed questions. It involves looking at all aspects of your life with an openness to rework nutrition, exercise, schedules, and digging into your heart to see if you are fulfilled with yourself and your family. It is about asking yourself what your money story is, and how to get it in alignment with what you want for your life.

The five pillars to making a change are:

1. Courage: You know you are more scared to stay where you are than to step forward into the unknown.
2. Choice: This is in your ultimate power.
3. Connection: To make a change, you must understand what you want to be in your own life. When you make that decision, you can connect with others by asking for support in making the change happen.
4. Creation: Depending on the change, we have to get creative, plan and be goal-oriented to make the change successful.
5. Community: Whenever we make one change to our life, it does have a ripple effect on ourselves, others and beyond. It might be that we are happier, which ripples to our kids, teams, clients and the world.

Our hope for you is that you take the rawness and realness of these stories and reflect on how you can define and achieve a kind of balance that is in alignment with your best life.

Join our Facebook group

https:www.facebook.com/groups/getyouvisible

Do You Dream of Being a Published

Author?

The best part of what I do is bringing people together to write, share, and inspire those that may feel alone or in need of healing. Your story could help to heal others.

My team will guide you through the writing process, so your idea can become a reality to be shared on worldwide distribution channels.

A book has been referenced as an authority piece for centuries and is known to be one of the best ways to gain instant credibility and visibility with clients in the online and offline space.

If you have a story to share and want to become a published author, then let's talk. Here's to your story and someone waiting to read it.

Book your complimentary call with me.

www.getyouvisible.com

Join us:

https://www.facebook.com/groups/getyouvisiblecommunity

See you on the other side.

Heather Andrews

CEO, Get You Visible

CPSIA information can be obtained
at www.ICGtesting.com
Printed in the USA
LVHW050436200820
663575LV00007B/371